Mountain West Foraging for Beginners

Unlocking Nature's Pantry in a Breathtaking Region – A Practical Field Guide to Wild Edibles

Table of Contents

Introduction

Foraging – combing the wilderness for nature's edibles – is a skill that is largely forgotten in the modern, supermarket-driven world. In Mountain West Foraging for Beginners, the aim is to reignite that ancient knowledge and show you how easy, fun, and delicious foraging can be, even if you've never set foot in the wilderness. Nearly every plant in the Mountain West region has some culinary or medicinal use; you just need to know how to identify and harvest them properly.

Foraging, in and of itself, is exciting. One minute, you're strolling through the woods; the next, you're unearthing a motherlode of wild blueberries or spotting a cluster of morel mushrooms peeking through the soil. It's how you connect with the land and discover the plants and flavors that have sustained humans for millennia. Sure, the wilderness might be intimidating, even perilous, especially for the uninitiated. That's why the focus here is getting beginners out into nature with confidence. You won't be bogged down with scientific jargon or long lists of scary-sounding Latin names. Instead, you'll find beautifully illustrated plant profiles complete with clear identification tips, ethical harvesting methods, and, of course, easy but tasty recipes.

Curious about how to tell a matsutake from a death cap? Drowning in a sea of green leaves and not sure which ones you can eat? Don't worry about it – you're getting simple ID guides and techniques tailored to the plants of the American West. By the end of this book, you'll know how and where to find wild berries, acorns, and edible mushrooms without fear of making a life-threatening mistake.

Many wild plants also have the most shocking medicinal properties. Did you know that yarrow leaves could be used to make a soothing skin salve? Or that the horsetail can literally save your life if you ever get into a real-life version of Man vs. Wild? The mountains, forests, and prairies of the American West are teeming with free, incredibly useful plants just waiting for you to find them – if only you knew where to look. Ditch the grocery store and reconnect with the land. With this book, the wilderness will start to feel a lot less intimidating and a whole lot more breathtaking (in a good way).

Chapter 1: Foraging in the Mountain West: Getting Started

The Mountain West? Isn't that just a bunch of, you know, mountains? You couldn't be more wrong. The Mountain West is a land of contrasts; there's so much more to this rugged region than meets the eye. To really understand what the Mountain West is, imagine standing at the base of a towering, snow-capped peak, its jagged summit piercing the sky like the fangs of some ancient, slumbering beast. It's enough to make you feel small, but in the best way, you know? These giants have stood vigil over the land for centuries, their stones guarding the secrets of the plants and creatures that call this place home.

Explore the Mountain West to forage a diverse collection of plants, fungi, and more.[1]

As you descend from those heights and into the thick, verdant forests, it's almost a completely different world. The canopy of tall pines, firs, and aspens filters the sunlight, creating this peaceful, almost mystical atmosphere. If you look closely, you start to notice all these beautiful plants and mysterious-looking fungi hiding among the roots and mossy undergrowth, waiting for the curious forager – waiting for you.

Sprinkled throughout this natural landscape, you also have the arid, wind-swept deserts, where life has found a way to thrive in the most inhospitable of conditions. Uneven canyons and vast, empty stretches of land give way to oases of lush greenery fed by hidden springs and aquifers. It's a land of extremes, where the line between desolation and abundance is drawn razor-thin. The Mountain West is a forager's playground that promises to surprise, enchant, and test you.

Overview of the Mountain West's Edible Bounty

Suppose you've ever been hiking or camping in the mountains of the American West. In that case, you've probably stumbled across all sorts of wild edibles growing around you. This scenic region is home to a surprising abundance of wild, natural foods that have sustained local populations for more years than you can possibly imagine. Of course, you'll need to know what you're looking for to safely indulge in nature's provisions. In the Mountain West, you'll find:

- **Berries:** Berries are small, juicy fruits that grow on low shrubs or vines. They're usually bite-sized, with a sweet or tart flavor. Mountain berries are no exception; they come in loads and loads of colors and flavors. Some of the most common wild berries you'll find in the Mountain West are huckleberries, serviceberries, gooseberries, thimbleberries, kinnikinnick (bearberries), etc. These berries are an important food source for all the critters, from bears and deer to birds and small mammals, including humans. You have to be really careful when foraging for wild berries, though. Some lookalike species could be poisonous, so absolute certainty could save your life. The availability of wild berries in the mountains also varies a lot from year to year, depending on factors like rainfall and temperature. Some seasons overflow with berries, while the crop is slim in other years. That's part of what makes it special when you do find them.

- **Mushrooms:** Mushrooms are the fleshy, spore-bearing fruiting bodies of fungi that grow in soil, on decaying matter, or in symbiotic relationships with plants. Some of the most common and notable mushroom types in this region are porcini, chanterelles, morels, lobster mushrooms, chicken of the woods, and so on. Many mountain mushrooms, like the porcini and chanterelle, have a special relationship with trees. They connect their roots in a mutually beneficial partnership, trading nutrients and water. Other mushrooms, like morels and chicken of the woods, have a different job description. They break down dead plant and animal matter, recycling those nutrients back into the soil. You can imagine how important this decomposition is for the productivity of the mountain environment. The availability of wild mushrooms can be pretty unpredictable from year to year, considering factors like rainfall, temperature, and even wildfires. Rainy, mild summers typically mean a lot of mushrooms, while drought or extreme heat leads to slim pickings. To forage for wild mushrooms, being an expert on identification is an absolute must. Many mountain mushroom species have extremely poisonous lookalikes. You're looking at severe illness or even death if you eat the wrong one. Experienced mushroom hunters rely on field guides, phone apps, and local mycology experts to ensure they have the right fungi. They closely examine details like the mushroom's gills, spore color, and cap shape to confirm the ID. On the bright side, mountain mushrooms aren't just delicious; many also have impressive medicinal properties as long as you pick the right ones.

- **Nuts and Seeds:** One of the most famous nuts from this region is the pine nut. Also called pinyon nuts, these guys come from various species of pine trees found all over the Rockies and Cascades. Another mountain nut worth mentioning is the hazelnut, or filbert, as they're sometimes called. While not quite as common as pine nuts, wild hazelnuts grow in mountain shrublands and forests, especially in the Pacific Northwest. Beyond nuts, the mountains are also home to some edible wild seeds. Sunflower seeds are probably the most well-known. These grow on tall sunflower plants dotting prairies, meadows, and mountainsides. Another interesting wild seed is from a plant called the Rocky Mountain beeweed, also known as Cleome. This plant's small, peppery seeds were gathered and eaten by tribes like the Utes and Pueblos, who also used the leaves and flowers for food and medicine. Naturally, you have to be careful when foraging for any wild foods, including nuts and seeds. Some varieties found in the mountains could be poisonous if you eat them, and even with the safe, edible types, you need to harvest responsibly. Taking too many nuts or seeds will interfere with the mountain ecosystems and leave wildlife without an important food source. A little moderation goes a long way when enjoying what nature has to offer.

- **Plants:** At the very highest elevations, where the air is thin and the temperatures are freezing, you'll find the tough and resilient plants of the Mountain West. Plants like the Indian paintbrush are specially adapted to survive the harsh, windy conditions up in the alpine zone. They grow really low to the ground to conserve heat and moisture. As you hike down the mountainsides, the plant life changes dramatically. Engelmann spruce, subalpine fir, and white bark pine trees dominate the landscape in the subalpine forests. Down in their shady understories, you'll spot plants like kinnikinnick, bunchberry, and twinflower getting by on the dappled sunlight.

Further down the slopes, the forests become more mixed, with ponderosa pines, Douglas firs, and quaking aspens growing alongside trees like Gambel oak and bigtooth maple. The forest floors here are carpeted with all kinds of lush ferns, colorful wildflowers, and berry bushes.

Finally, at the lowest elevations, there are open grassland prairies and scrubby shrublands. These sun-loving habitats are home to drought-tolerant plants like blazing stars, prickly pear, gaillardia, yucca, and sagebrush. They've evolved special adaptations to survive in the Mountain West's hot, dry summers. All of these mountain plants provide food and shelter for countless animals, help regulate soil and water resources, and are deeply woven into the cultural traditions of the region's Indigenous peoples. Sadly, they are facing some big challenges these days. Habitats are being destroyed, invasive species are moving in, droughts are worsening, and wildfires are burning hotter and more frequently.

Everyone needs to come together to do their part to appreciate and conserve these special places. Just learning about the plants that live there is a great start. They aren't just pretty faces; they're the backbone of entire ecosystems. When you see them as the living, breathing members of the mountain community that they are, it changes how you view and interact with these spaces. The more you do to safeguard these habitats, the better chance they have of living long into the future.

Engelmann spruce.[2]

Historical Significance of Foraging

Anyone who spends time in the high country of the American West – it doesn't have to be a forager – might notice people out in the woods and meadows carefully picking berries, gathering nuts and seeds, or hunting for mushrooms. This practice of foraging for wild, edible plants has deep roots in the region. In fact, it's been an integral part of life for the Indigenous tribes of the Mountain West for thousands of years.

Long before European settlers ever arrived, the Native peoples of Colorado, Utah, Montana, and beyond were intimately familiar with the wild foods that could be sustainably harvested from the natural environment. For tribes like the Utes, Arapahos, Shoshones, and Pueblos, foraging was more than just a way to put food on the table – it was a sacred cultural tradition passed down through the generations.

The women of these tribes were often the primary foragers, developing extensive knowledge about when and where to find the ripest huckleberries, juiciest serviceberries, or freshest mushrooms. Certain wild plants were even used in spiritual ceremonies and traditional medicines. At the time, foraging was seen as a means to connect with the land and honor its abundance.

Sadly, when European colonizers arrived and forcibly removed Native Americans from their ancestral homelands, these ancient foraging traditions were nearly lost. As tribes were confined to reservations and their access to traditional food sources was restricted, the deep connection between mountain people and the wild bounty of their environment was severely thrown off.

Luckily for the world, the knowledge and practices of Indigenous mountain foragers never disappeared completely. In recent decades, there's been a real resurgence of interest in traditional wild food harvesting within Native American communities and the broader public. This "wild foods movement" is driven by a growing awareness of the environmental, economic, and health benefits of rediscovering local, sustainable food sources.

These days, organizations like the Native American Food Sovereignty Alliance are working hard to revive ancestral plant knowledge and help tribal members regain access to their homelands' increasingly threatened wild foods. Meanwhile, environmentally conscious consumers search for wild-gathered berries, nuts, and mushrooms as healthy, ethical alternatives to industrialized agriculture. When foraging is done sustainably, selective harvesting of certain plants can help maintain the diversity and resilience of mountain ecosystems. It's a return to the time-honored Indigenous principle of living in harmony with the land rather than exploiting it.

Practical Tips for Novices

As a newbie forager who wants to try their hand at harvesting wild edibles in the mountains, you might have questions, be confused, or even consider giving up and just driving to the supermarket. It's normal; no one is judging. With so many different plants, mushrooms, berries, and nuts growing out there, how do you even know what's safe to eat? Well, it's a good thing you're here because with the right preparation and a commitment to responsible learning, even complete beginners like you can go out there and return home safely with a bag full of food.

The trick to successful and safe foraging is plant identification. Accurately recognizing edible species – and, just as importantly, telling them apart from any poisonous lookalikes – is essential. Really, it's a matter of life and death. That's why good field guides are still selling out. Look for a regional guide with detailed illustrations and descriptions of the wild foods found in your specific area, Colorado, Montana, Utah, or elsewhere.

When using a field guide, pay close attention to each plant's little identifying characteristics, like the shape of the leaves, the type of flowers or fruit it produces, the structure of the stem, and the habitat where it grows. Don't just rely on one or two features; cross-reference multiple traits to make a positive ID. It's also good to learn about how plants change through the seasons since the same species can look quite different at different times of the year.

On top of the visual cues, your other senses will also help with plant recognition. Try crushing or squeezing the leaves or stems to pick up on the scent, texture, and even subtle flavors. Be very careful about tasting anything until you're 100% sure you have the right plant. Another important skill is learning to track the seasonal patterns and peak abundance times for different wild edibles in your area. Edibles like berries, nuts, and mushrooms perform exceptionally well at certain elevations and in specific habitats, reaching their prime ripeness at different points throughout the year. Environmental clues – like when leaves start budding or flowers start blooming – will help you anticipate where and when to find your foraging targets.

Naturally, you should also be aware of responsible, sustainable harvesting practices. You never want to over-pick or damage wild plant populations. A forager knows to only take what they need, leave plenty for the wildlife, and never uproot entire plants. Forage with reverence, patience, and humility. This ancient skill takes time and study to master, so start small, rely on trustworthy resources, *and always err on the side of caution.*

The Ethical Responsibility of Mountain Foragers

As more and more people get excited about harvesting wild, natural foods, an awareness program should be in place to educate the public on environmental responsibility and care. If done without proper consideration, foraging has the potential to throw the mountain ecosystem out of balance, but if you approach it with respect and wholehearted investment in sustainable practices, you could contribute to the preservation of the health and biodiversity of these precious landscapes.

Before you even think about gathering anything to eat, you need to be sure you can recognize not just the edible species but also any endangered plants and key species vital to the mountain environment. Skipping this crucial step of thorough research and learning is a big no-no. Even if a wild plant seems abundant, over-picking can still excessively deplete the local population and interrupt the cycle that sustains the whole ecosystem. A responsible forager always leaves the majority of any given resource for wildlife and future human harvesters.

Besides, it's not just about how much you take; how you gather matters, too. Uprooting entire plants, breaking branches, or scarring tree bark will cause lasting damage. Instead, use tools judiciously and only collect the specific parts you need, like leaves, fruits, or mushroom caps, while leaving the core structure intact.

Beyond the actual foraging itself, you must also be thoughtful about where you're sourcing your wild foods. Getting permission to access private lands, avoiding protected natural areas, and steering clear of polluted sites are all necessary considerations. Trampling sensitive habitats or over-harvesting in one location will deprive wildlife, erode public trust, and jeopardize future access for the whole foraging community. Ethical foragers see themselves as a steward and caretaker of the land, not just an extractor of their bounty. This attitude is built on an ongoing, intimate engagement with natural cycles and a genuine appreciation for the generosity of the ecosystems that provide you sustenance.

Ethical foragers see themselves as a steward and caretaker of the land, not just an extractor of their bounty.[3]

Now that you have the basics down on foraging in the mountains, it's safe to say that you're in for a treat. Soon enough, you'll understand why foragers say that foraging is about so much more than just filling your belly. You become connected to the cycles of mountain ecosystems, the ageless traditions of Indigenous peoples, and your own primal roots as a human being, and that is only the beginning. After you learn to harvest and prepare your harvest with care, your diet becomes noticeably healthy, locally sourced, and eco-conscious. The next few chapters will familiarize you with the diversity of wild edibles found in the mountain regions of the West. Prepare for the discovery of the wilderness around you and of yourself as a part of it.

Chapter 2: Foraging Tools, Equipment, and Safety

Foraging is not without its risks. Before you start randomly plucking and popping things in your mouth, you're going to need the right tools and a safety protocol. Life in the wild isn't all fun and games; there are some very real risks if you don't know what you're doing. Mistaking a toxic plant for an edible one could land you in the hospital, and getting lost in the wilderness is not an experience you want to have. In this chapter, you'll learn everything you need to know about the essential gear and best practices to forage efficiently and, most importantly, without ending up in the emergency room.

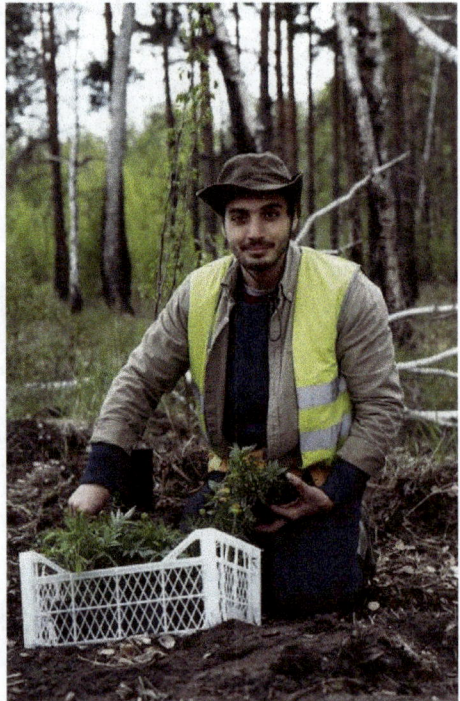

You need the right tools and a safety protocol to safely forage.‘

The Importance of Proper Preparation and Responsible Foraging

- **Your Health and Safety Come First:** It cannot be stressed enough how critical it is to learn everything you can about a plant's ID before you start foraging. Misidentifying a toxic lookalike could end you up in a hospital or worse. This could mean nausea, vomiting, and potentially even organ failure. Not exactly the "natural high" you were going for, isn't it? Commit time to studying field guides, taking workshops, and consulting with local experts. Learn to recognize not just the edible parts but also the plant's leaves, stems, and flowers. Do your homework and always play it safe.

- **Don't Compromise on Gear:** You've already covered the life-saving importance of accurate plant identification, but do not forget your safety gear. A strong field knife, foraging basket, and first-aid kit could be the difference between a nice time and a trip to the ER. Invest in the right tools, and your foraging experiences will be far less "extreme."

- **Timing Is Everything:** Wild edibles' nutritional value and palatability will fluctuate dramatically throughout the season. Harvest at the wrong time, and you might end up with something bitter, woody, or even poisonous. Respect the rhythms of nature and do your research to determine the optimal windows for collecting different plants and fungi.

- **Sustainability Is Key:** Responsible foraging means *only taking* what you need and leaving the rest to regenerate. Grab only a small portion of the available berries or mushrooms and move on. This ensures a plentiful harvest for years to come, both for you and the local wildlife. It's similar to pruning a fruit tree; you trim just enough to encourage new growth, not hack it down to the stump.

- **Respect the Land and Its Keepers:** The land you're foraging on may hold cultural, spiritual, or historical significance for Indigenous communities. Proceed with respect, tread lightly, and be informed of any local protocols or regulations. After all, *you're a guest there,* so act accordingly. Mother Nature doesn't take kindly to disrespect.

Understanding and Preparing for the Rugged Terrain

Every hiker who has been to the Rockies will tell you that the Mountain West is a high-stakes, high-intensity environment. One minute, you're walking along a nice trail, and the next, you're clinging to the side of a cliff, wondering how the heck you're going to get back down.

Mountain West foragers are the true masters of that landscape, moving through the peaks and valleys with a certain grace and agility, but make no mistake, surviving in this wilderness is not as easy as they make it look. These people are part mountain goat, part wilderness expert, and part adrenaline junkie. The slopes are steep and crumbling, and the weather is so unpredictable that it could go from sunny skies to blizzards in a flash. Throw in the occasional encounter with some less-than-friendly local wildlife, and any regular person would rather stay home, but you're not regular, are you? You want to feel the rush of outsmarting Mother Nature at her own game. After all, what's the point of roaming one of the most jagged, unpredictable environments on the planet if you can't have a little fun with it, right?

To make it as a Mountain West forager, you must be quick on your feet, sharp as a tack, and blessed with the balance of a Cirque du Soleil performer. Here is why:

- Knowing the Lay of the Land

  When you're out there in the mountains, you should know how to read the landscape like the back of your hand. Foragers need to be able to recognize key landmarks, understand how the slopes and terrain will affect their travel, and identify potential hazards or obstacles along their path. This groundwork helps them plan the safest and most efficient routes and avoid getting into trouble.

- Have the Right Gear and Skills

  Going into the mountains requires some specialized know-how and equipment. Foragers need to be trained in techniques like climbing over rocky outcrops or scaling snowy slopes. Having the right gear, like crampons for icy areas or snowshoes for deep powder, could quite literally determine whether you make it back home.

- Adapt to the Seasons

  In the Mountain West, the environment is in constant flux, with dramatic changes from one season to the next. What works in the summer heat may be completely useless in the dead of winter. Foragers must be ready to adjust their strategies, shelter, and clothing to match the current conditions. Flexibility is necessary for your survival.

- Dealing with Wild Neighbors

  As a forager, you'll run into wild animals at some point and need to know how to handle those encounters. Animals get aggressive if you tamper with their food, make sudden movements around them, or get too close to their young or their territory. You must learn to identify the different species, know the best ways to scare them away and have a plan for what to do if one of them decides to attack.

- Identify and Manage the Risks

  Danger lurks around every corner of the mountains. Foragers need a sharp eye for possible threats. That means closely monitoring the weather, checking the snowpack's stability, and being alert for any signs of dangerous animals. Assessing the risks ahead of time and taking smart precautions will get you back home safely.

- Share Knowledge and Work Together

  No one person knows it all. That's why experienced foragers share their hard-earned wisdom with newcomers and why groups often work together. Tapping into this collective knowledge and support network will give you a major advantage.

Essential Foraging Tools

- **Pocket Knife:** A good pocket knife is your best friend out in the wild mountain forests. This is your all-purpose tool. It has a sharp blade for cutting and slicing your finds, plus handy extras like scissors and screwdrivers. Buy one that is sturdy and rust-resistant, and make sure it's lightweight enough that you don't mind carrying it around all day.

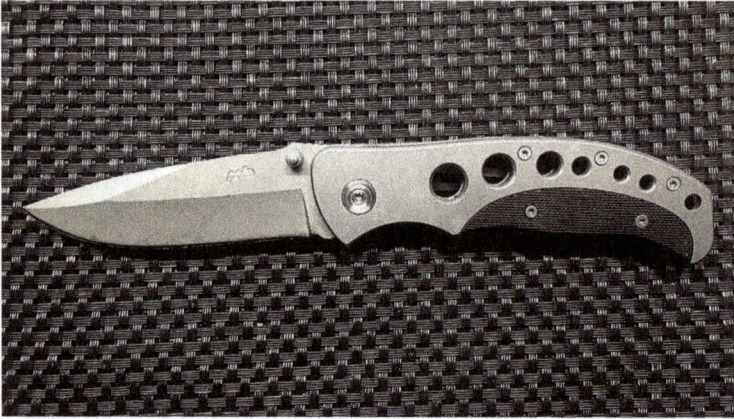

Pocket knife.[5]

- **Foraging Basket:** Your foraging bag or basket is where you'll stash your finds. Look for one made of tough, natural materials like woven straw or canvas. It should have a comfortable strap or handle so your hands are free to keep searching. Also, try to find one with different compartments – that way, you can keep your berries separate from your mushrooms, for example, and everything stays nice and fresh.

Foraging basket.[6]

- **Field Guide:** Before heading out, pack a good field guide or download a plant identification app. These will be your lifesavers, helping you tell the difference between the safe and the dangerous plants. The guides cover all the local plants in detail, with pictures and descriptions, so you can quickly figure out what's safe to eat. Spend some time learning how to use these resources so that when you're out there, you'll be able to identify your finds on the spot.

- **Compass and Map:** A compass and map are important for staying oriented in the mountains. The map shows the trails, landmarks, and potential pitfalls. Learn how to use them together so you can always find your way back. Protect them from the elements by laminating the map or putting it in a waterproof case.

Compass and map.[7]

- **Survival Kit:** In the wilderness, you never know what might happen. That's why a survival kit is indispensable. Pack the essentials: a fire starter, an emergency blanket, a whistle, and first-aid supplies. Customize your kit to the mountain environment you're exploring, and keep it in a waterproof container so everything stays dry and ready to use if you need it.

- **Pruning Shears:** For tougher or thicker plants, you'll want a good pair of pruning shears or a folding saw. Pick one with sharp, durable blades that can handle the job without wearing down. If it comes with a locking mechanism, it's even better. It'll keep your fingers safe while you're cutting.

Pruning shears.°

- **Water Bottle:** Hydration is mandatory when you're out foraging. Bring a water bottle that won't leak, and pair it with a water filtration system. That way, you can refill the water from the streams and rivers and know that the water is clean and safe to drink.

Safety as a Top Priority

Rule number one?

Never (seriously), never go foraging solo.

The risks are simply too high. You need a trustworthy person by your side. You might be happily picking wild nuts out there, and then, BAM, you twist your ankle! You can't even stand up, or maybe you accidentally stumble into a patch of stinging nettles. Your whole body erupts in angry red welts. Without a partner there to help you, you're stranded. You could be lying in the middle of the woods for hours or even days before someone finally realizes you're missing, and by that point, the outcome probably won't be too pleasant.

A foraging friend is your insurance policy. They can administer first-aid, call for emergency services if necessary (hopefully not), and even just keep you company to stave off the creepy-crawly forest feeling. You can share your foraging finds, swap identification tips, and make a day of it. Plus, having an extra set of eyes and hands around is just plain safer.

Next on the safety checklist is gear, gear, and more gear. You're going to want to pack like you're heading out on a full-blown wilderness expedition because, in a way, that's exactly what you're doing. Water, energy bars, rope, a flashlight – the whole nine yards. Navigation tools are also an absolute must. The old-fashioned map and compass are great, but a GPS device is even better. You don't want to be that person who gets hopelessly lost, wandering in circles until you finally collapse from exhaustion.

Speaking of collapsing, a comprehensive first-aid kit is a necessity. Bandages, antiseptics, pain relievers, antihistamines – the works. You never know when you might encounter a bad scrape, a bee sting, or even a serious allergic reaction. Better to have it and not need it than the other way around, and for the love of all things edible, make sure you know exactly what you're foraging. Bring a field guide or download a plant ID app.

Keep an eye out for any possible hazards, like slippery terrain, angry insects, or the dreaded poison ivy. You do not want to be scratching and sneezing your way through the woods. Last but not least, let someone know your plan before you head out. Give them your route and your expected return time, and tell them to sound the alarm if you're not back when you said you would be. You want a search party, not missing person posters.

Appropriate Clothing

Proper attire is non-negotiable for a safe and comfortable foraging trip. You want to make sure you're dressed for the elements and the terrain you'll be exploring.

Let's start from ground level: Closed-toe footwear is mandatory. Hiking boots or rugged sneakers with good traction are ideal. Anything less, and you're just asking for a sprained ankle or a nasty cut on your foot. Nobody wants to be hobbling through the wilderness because they thought it'd be good to forage in flip-flops!

Moving upward: Long pants are highly recommended to protect your legs. You'll be pushing through thick vegetation, brambles, and who knows what else. Exposed skin is vulnerable to scratches, stings, and potential exposure to poison ivy or other irritants. Tuck your pant legs into your boots for an extra layer of defense.

For your upper body: Opt for long sleeves. Again, this will shield you from scratches, bug bites, and other unpleasantness. Natural fiber materials like cotton or linen are breathable and offer good coverage. Stay away from delicate fabrics that could easily get snagged or torn. Suppose you're heading into an area with ticks or other biting insects. In that case, you may want to consider wearing permethrin-treated clothing. This odorless, invisible insect repellent will give you an extra layer of defense against insects, especially the disease-carrying variety.

Don't forget sun protection! A wide-brimmed hat and UV-blocking sunglasses will keep the sun out of your eyes and prevent sunburn. Slathering on some high-SPF sunscreen (nothing less than SPF 30) is also highly advised, especially if you'll be out foraging for long hours.

For your sake, suit up in a way that shields your body from the many hazards you may run into while foraging. It may not be the most fashionable look, but you'll be thanking yourself when you come out of the woods unscathed.

Additional Equipment

- **Gloves:** Gloves are arguably one of the most important pieces of equipment a forager can have. Your bare hands could easily get scratched, cut, or exposed to irritants. Gloves keep them protected, so you can poke around without overthinking it. They also let you really examine the plants and fungi you want to forage. You can hold and look at the leaves, stems, and other details up close without accidentally damaging delicate specimens. This attention to detail is key to making sure you ID things correctly. Different gloves work great for foraging. Breathable work gloves with good grip are a popular choice. Some people prefer thinner, more nimble gloves with equal protection. For mushroom hunting, cut-resistant gloves are a smart pick. Aim for a balance of dexterity, durability, and coverage for what you need.

Use gloves to safely forage.[9]

- **Magnifying Glass:** With a good magnifier, you can scrutinize leaf patterns, stem structures, spore colors, and other key ID features that might be tricky to see with just your eyeballs. Foraging guides and field books are great, but having that added visual magnification is even better. Buy one with sufficient magnifying power. At least 10x is recommended for reliable identification.

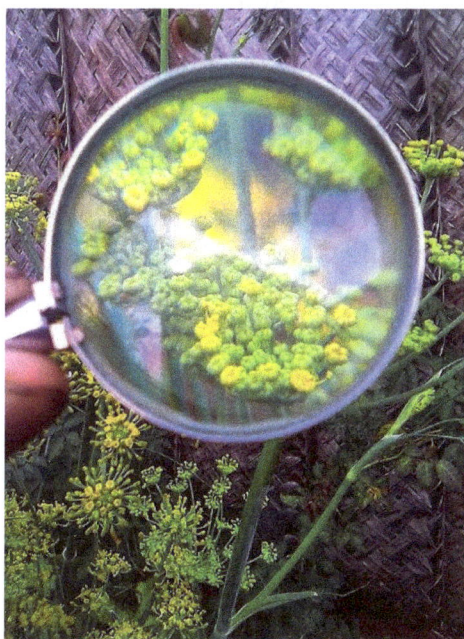

Magnifying glass.[10]

- **Containers:** There are a few different options for foragers. Mesh baskets are great for delicate finds like mushrooms, berries, and leaves. The breathable design helps prevent suffocation and allows for airflow. A paper bag or cardboard box might be your best bet for something a little tougher, like roots, nuts, or fruits. They will protect your haul from getting crushed while still leaving room for proper air circulation. Extra tip: bring a small cooler or insulated bag to keep things chilled, particularly if you're collecting perishable items like mushrooms or greens. The last thing you want to deal with is a slimy, wilted mess by the time you get home.

Tips on Maintaining and Caring for Tools

- Clean Your Tools

  After you're done foraging, clean all the tools. Use a stiff brush and some mild soap and water to remove any dirt, plant bits, or other gunk that has built up. Dry them off completely when you're done because you don't want rusty equipment.

- Sharpen Your Blades

  Dull blades are the worst; they make foraging much harder than it needs to be. Get yourself a good sharpening stone or file and learn how to use it properly. Buy one with both coarse and fine grit surfaces. Start with the coarser side to reshape that dull edge quickly and get it looking sharp again. Then, move it to the fine side to really refine and polish that cutting edge until it's razor-sharp. The proper sharpening technique requires the right angle. For most foraging knives, that's usually between 20 and 30 degrees. If you're not sure, feel free to use a sharpening guide. This guarantees you're sharpening the blade, not accidentally grinding it down.

  As you're sharpening, concentrate on using a consistent, smooth stroke. Gently pull the blade across the stone at that same angle, avoiding too much pressure. Putting too much force behind it will just end up damaging the edge you're trying to sharpen. Finish up by honing the edge on a nice, smooth steel rod. This will further refine and align that cutting surface, making it as precise and keen as possible.

- Rust Prevention

  Moisture is the enemy of every metal tool. Prevent rust by thoroughly drying all your tools after use and applying a light coat of food-grade mineral oil or rust-preventative spray. If you'll be storing them for a long time, wrap the metal parts in acid-free paper or place silica gel packs nearby.

- Wooden Handle Care

  For tools with wooden handles, rub the handles down with a food-safe oil like linseed, tung, or walnut oil. This conditions the wood to prevent drying and cracking – and helps ensure a secure grip. *Don't use vegetable oils because they get rancid!*

- Moving Parts

  Tools with hinges, springs, and other moving bits require extra TLC. They need to be cleaned, lubricated, and checked regularly. Use a stiff brush to sweep away any dirt and debris in those mechanisms. Then, give a drop or two of lightweight machine oil for smooth movement.

  After every cleaning and oiling, do a quick function test. Ensure those hinges open and close easily and the springs give the right amount of tension. If something feels stuck or loose, deal with it right away before it becomes a bigger problem.

- Regular Inspection

  Catch problems before they catch you. Before and after every foraging trip, you'll want to give your tools a thorough once-over. Look for any nicks, cracks, or signs of wear and tear, especially in high-stress areas like where the blade meets the handle. If you find anything starting to go south, it's time to repair or replace that part. There is no point in risking life and limb with sketchy equipment.

- Replace Worn-Out Parts

  Even if you're the ultimate tool caretaker meticulously cleaning, sharpening, and caring for your gear, eventually, things will start wearing down. It's just the nature of the beast. Those parts and materials can only take so much abuse out in the field. Stay vigilant for any signs of wear and tear. Worn-out springs may not bounce back, screws might have worked themselves loose, handles may be cracked or splintered, and blades might not hold an edge no matter how much you sharpen them. These are all indicators that it's time to start sourcing some replacement parts. Cheap, generic parts might seem like a deal at the moment, but they're likely to wear out even faster than the originals. Get the right replacement parts for your specific make and model, and don't be afraid to spend a little extra for durability and reliability. The sooner you swap out the tired, worn-out components, the sooner you'll get back outdoors with a tool that's less likely to disappoint you.

In the end, caring for your tools is only half the battle. As a responsible forager, you are obligated to care for the land and resources you're siphoning. That means always adhering to the principle of leaving no trace. Pack out everything you pack in, move carefully, and don't even attempt anything that could damage or disturb the natural environment. Take *only what you need*, and do NOT overharvest. Different regions have different rules in place to guarantee the long-term sustainability of foraging. Abide by those guidelines not only for legal reasons but because it's the responsible thing to do.

Chapter 3: Seasonal Foraging in the Mountain West

The Mountain West changes with the seasons and the calendar, and the menu of the wilderness changes along with it. In spring, the first signs of life wake up after winter. Flowers and bushes come up from under the ground to brighten up the meadows. Summer brings a riot of green everywhere you look. The mountainsides are enveloped in thick forests, and the valleys are covered in wildflowers. Streams and rivers rise with melting snow, and the bees, butterflies, and other pollinators busily move from blossom to blossom, ensuring all the plants produce their seeds and berries. As fall rolls around, the cycle shifts again.

The Mountain West changes with the seasons and the calendar, and the menu of the wilderness changes along with it.[11]

The leaves turn brilliant shades before dropping to the ground, returning their nutrients to the soil. The grasses and flowers turn their energy inward, and the pace of life slows as even the animals prepare for the cold. It is winter again, a quieter, more introspective season, a time of dormancy before the cycle starts again. Regardless of the circumstances, the forager moves in harmony with the land, reading the cycles of nature and connecting to the ever-turning wheel of the seasons. There is always something to find, something to harvest, and something to appreciate, but only for the alert, the wise, and the patient.

Spring

Spring brings a dramatic transformation to the Mountain West. For months, the region has been blanketed in a thick layer of snow, with bare trees and dormant plants as far as the eye can see, but as the weather warms up, all that begins to change. The snow gradually melts, revealing the uneven, rocky terrain that defines this part of the country. The massive mountain peaks that were once completely white begin to show their true colors again, with patches of gray, brown, and tan peeking through the receding snow. Down in the valleys, the melting snow reveals the dirt and soil underneath, preparing for the return of plant life, and that's when things really get interesting.

The sagebrush is one of the first plants you'll notice making a comeback. Its distinctive silvery-green leaves reappear, signaling the arrival of spring. Soon after, other plants begin to push up through the thawing ground, more than happy to take advantage of the warming temperatures and increased sunlight.

You'll see a few edible wild greens and vegetables in the lower elevations and valleys. Miner's lettuce is one of them. It reappears in spring, sprawling across the forest floor in beautiful green patches. Dandelion greens also make an appearance, along with currants, chickweed, and wild onions.

Moving into the more forested areas, you might be lucky enough to see another springtime favorite: the morel mushroom. These fungi emerge as the snow melts at higher elevations, typically popping up in clusters around the bases of trees. Morels have a distinctive, honeycomb-like cap and an unmistakable earthy flavor that foragers and chefs simply love.

Obviously, the return of plant life isn't the only sign of spring in the Mountain West. As the snow continues to melt, the streams and rivers that wind through the valleys start to flow again. After being frozen solid for months, the clear, cold water rushes and tumbles over the rocky beds. The reactivation of these waterways brings back the wildlife that had been forced to find shelter deeper in the forests during the harsh winter months. Mule deer and bighorns will be seen grazing on the new growth, and smaller animals like pikas and ground squirrels will also come out of their burrows, scurrying around in search of food and sunlight. Overhead, the skies are once again filled with the sounds of birds returning from their winter homes. Songbirds like the mountain bluebird and the yellow-rumped warbler dart from tree to tree, singing. Even the raptors, like golden eagles, come out of hiding to soar high above the mountain peaks in search of prey. It is spring, and the world is coming back to life.

Tips for Foraging in Spring

- The spring foraging season in the Mountain West typically runs from April through June, with the peak happening in May.

- Elevation is important. Lower elevations will have earlier springs, while higher mountain areas may still have snow well into May or June.

- Be aware of bears, mountain lions, and other wildlife that may be active in the spring.

- The mornings are usually the best time to go foraging in spring, between about 8 and 11 a.m. The plants are fresher, and the weather is milder.

- Dress in layers, and bring rain gear and sun protection. The temperature swings a lot between day and night.

- Take it easy on fragile or slow-growing spring plants that might not recover well from heavy harvesting. Good examples are wild onions, bitterroot, wild strawberries, and morel mushrooms.

- Breathe deeply and let your nose guide you. Many wild edibles have a distinctive springtime smell when they're fresh. If something smells suspiciously nice, it could be worth investigating.

- Watch out for where birds, insects, and other animals are feeding. They're experts at finding the freshest spring plants.

- Don't forget to look up. Some of the best spring foraging can be found in the trees.

Summer

The long, warm days of spring gradually give way to the heat and abundance of summer. The snow covering the region for so many months has completely melted, revealing the terrain in all its glory. The transition to summer is a gradual process, but you know it's here because there is an explosion of plants and life.

The first sign of this change is the blooming of the Rocky Mountain columbines. You'll see this flower's purple, white, or pink varieties popping up all over the mountainsides. Right after, the meadows up in the mountains become more colorful than ever as flowers like the Indian paintbrush, sunflowers, and wild roses spread out all over the forest floor. For foragers, this is a time of plenty since there's a lot more to find now with the growth of wild plants and berries. Huckleberries, raspberries, and wild strawberries are some of the first to ripen.

Summer also brings many wild mushrooms for those with a bit more foraging experience. Chanterelles grow out from under the leaf litter in the cool, shaded areas of the forest. Boletes and oyster mushrooms can also be spotted on the sides of decaying logs.

Climbing higher into the mountains, the lavish meadows give way to the tough, low-growing plants of the alpine tundra. The land here is rough and sparse. You'll find the mountain avens, alpine bistrot, moss campion, and other plants that are specially adapted to intense sun, strong winds, and short growing seasons. Streams and rivers also flow through here, rushing down from the melting snow above.

Further up the mountains, *past the alpine zone*, the plants almost completely disappear, leaving bare rock, gravel, and glacial debris behind. This area belongs to the true alpine plants, like the alpine forget-me-not and the alpine sunflower, who somehow manage to cling to life on the steep, exposed mountainsides.

Alpine sunflower.[13]

Tips for Foraging in the Summer

- The best times to go foraging in the summer are the mornings, usually between 6 and 10 a.m.

- Some plants may completely shut down or die back in the heat, so you may have to adjust what you're looking for.

- The evenings after the sun goes down are also a good time to forage when it's cooler out.

- Bring lots of water and wear lightweight, breathable clothes to stay hydrated and comfortable in the heat.

- Some summer plants, like dandelion greens, wild spinach, stinging nettles, and purslane, may taste more bitter or unpalatable as the season goes on.

- Animals are great indicators of what is ripe and ready to harvest.

- Learn about edible mushrooms that fruit abundantly after heavy summer rains.

- Check south-facing slopes and sunny clearings because they usually have the highest concentration of summer berries and flowering plants.

Fall

As summer winds down and the weather gets cooler, the Mountain West enters the fall season. The days get shorter, and you can already feel the change in the air - a crispness that wasn't there just a few weeks ago. One of the most noticeable changes is the color of the landscape. The aspen trees along the mountainsides turn a beautiful golden yellow, and the evergreen conifers like pines and firs stay green - a contrast to the changing deciduous trees.

With the changing seasons also comes a change in the available harvest. High up in the forest, the nut-bearing trees like pines, firs, and spruces are dropping their edible pine nuts, while down lower, the oak trees are shedding their acorns.

For mushroom hunters, fall is an especially exciting time. While the summer days may have come with a variety of fungi, the porcini mushrooms come out in the fall. You'll find them growing at the base of trees or in the damp, shaded areas of the forest. Late-season berries like chokecherries and currants are also available during this season.

The temperatures continue to drop, and the wildlife starts its preparations for the coming winter. Moose and elk gather in large herds to graze the high meadows, fattening up before the snow arrives. Chipmunks and squirrels do their best to fill up their burrows for the long months ahead. Even birds notice the changing seasons, with many species making their way south in search of warmer areas. Birds of prey, like hawks and falcons, hunt for the last of the small animals before their own migration. Once alive with summer activity, the skies grow quieter as the songbirds leave, and the raptors are nowhere to be seen.

Tips for Foraging in the Fall

- Search for fall fruits, nuts, and seeds before small animals or the elements get to them first.
- Mild, sunny afternoons are usually the best time to go foraging in the fall.
- Early mornings are good when the plants are still holding on to that overnight dew or frost.
- Higher elevation sites will experience cooler temperatures and earlier frosts than the lower valleys, so plan accordingly.

- Try to harvest sensitive greens and herbs before the first frost causes them to wilt away.

- Don't take more than what you need. Leave plenty behind for the local wildlife.

- Note shortening daylight hours and plan your trips so you're not out too late.

- Try eating fall plant parts you might not normally think of, such as rose hips, cattail rhizomes, or pine needle tips.

Winter

As the first snowflakes drift down from the sky, the Mountain West turns into a world of white. The once-colorful valleys and hillsides are now shrouded in a thick layer of pristine snow. It is a very different place now. Foraging this season is definitely more complicated than the last three. With much of the terrain now buried beneath the frozen white, many of the edible plants have become inaccessible, out of reach. Yet, the resourceful forager understands that life is everywhere, even when it doesn't seem like it.

Down in the valleys and lower elevations, the snow often holds off until late fall, so in these areas, there are still pockets of green vegetation that survive the cold. If you look closely, you might see the leaves of wintercress, sorrel, chickweed, and, oddly enough, miner's lettuce poking through the snow – a much-appreciated source of fresh greens when everything else seems to have disappeared.

Many animals spend all year gathering and stashing away nuts to get them through the colder months, but some animals are more last-minute than others. They collect their nuts during the winter or just scavenge whatever they can find on the ground. This means two things for the forager: there are nuts in winter, and you can find them. All you have to do is find the right trees, and don't look up; look down and start excavating. For instance, fallen pinyon cones and nuts are easier to find against the backdrop of white snow. Simply follow the small animal tracks in the snow since they have already worked hard to find the best foraging spots for you.

For berries, the frost and snow help accelerate the ripening process, and at the same time, that chilly weather acts as a natural preservative, keeping them fresh longer than they'd last otherwise. Despite the harsh weather, you can still find blueberries, cranberries, lingonberries, and even some late-season raspberries. Winter may look dead and barren, but you will not go home empty-handed if you are observant and patient.

You can still find berries to forage in winter – despite the harsh weather.[18]

Tips for Foraging in Winter

- Funnel your efforts toward evergreen plants that are still green and accessible, like pine needles, spruce tips, or juniper berries

- Hardy, deep-rooted plants like burdock and sunchokes can still be dug up even when the ground is frozen

- Forage for animal signs like tracks, browse lines, or scats to get clues about what wild edibles the animals are finding

- Dress in warm, waterproof layers and watch your step on icy terrain

- Inspect the undersides of fallen logs and branches for signs of oysters or other cold-tolerant mushrooms

- Instead of searching for above-ground plants, dig into the snow to see what's available. There could be roots, vegetables, or edible bark

- Teaming up with experienced local foragers is not a bad idea

- Areas near water sources may have less snow cover and more accessible plants

Chapter 4: Wild Edible Plants of the Mountain West Region

This chapter will introduce you to a selection of the most easily recognizable and safe-to-eat wild plants found in the Mountain West, along with their characteristics, habitats, nutritional benefits, and a few extras. *As always, make sure to positively identify each plant before taking a bite, and avoid anything that looks even the slightest bit suspicious.*

When in doubt, it's best to just leave it alone.

That said, here are some of the wild plants of the Mountain West.

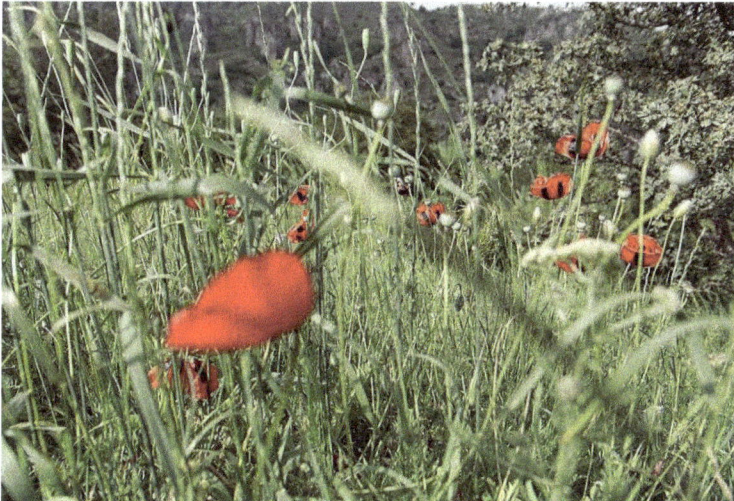

There are various wild plants that you can find in the Mountain West.[14]

Greens and Shoots

Dandelion Greens

Dandelion greens.[15]

- **Distinct Characteristics:** Dandelion greens are the leaves of the common dandelion *(Taraxacum officinale)*. They are quite variable in size and shape, anywhere from a couple of inches to nearly a foot long, but are often distinctively lobed with jagged, backward-facing "teeth".

- **Preferred Habitats:** Dandelions can be found growing in lawns, fields, and disturbed areas throughout the Mountain West.

- **Seasonal Nuances:** Dandelion greens will grow at almost any time of year, but are most common in spring. The young leaves are softest and have the best flavor, but larger and older leaves are still worth harvesting because they stand up to cooking better.

- **Nutritional Benefits:** Dandelion greens contain vitamins A, C, and K, iron, calcium, potassium, and fiber.

- **Identification Tips:** Dandelion leaves grow in a basal rosette directly from the ground without any visible stem. They have a very uneven, lobed appearance, like teeth along the leaf edges (where the plant gets its botanical name, Taraxacum, meaning "disorders of the teeth" in Greek). Dandelion "flowers" are really inflorescences, containing 12 to 25 strap-shaped "petals" that form a spherical bloom. These later develop into the signature dandelion "puffballs," spherical clusters of seed-bearing fluff.

- **Potential Lookalikes/Poisonous Counterparts:** Dandelions have no toxic lookalikes but other common (and edible) species in the sunflower family, like wild chicory or cat's ear (often called false dandelion), are similar enough to cause confusion. Look for plants with flowering stalks: dandelions have hollow, unbranched stalks that exude a milky sap.

Stinging Nettle (*Urtica dioica*)

- **Distinct Characteristics:**

  Stinging nettles (*Urtica dioica*) are large, perennial herbs with square stems reaching up to seven feet tall and serrated, teardrop-shaped leaves that are covered in tiny stinging hairs. The leaves are three to six inches long and oppositely arranged on the stems, and the plant's inconspicuous flowers emerge from the leaf axils in long catkin-like clusters.

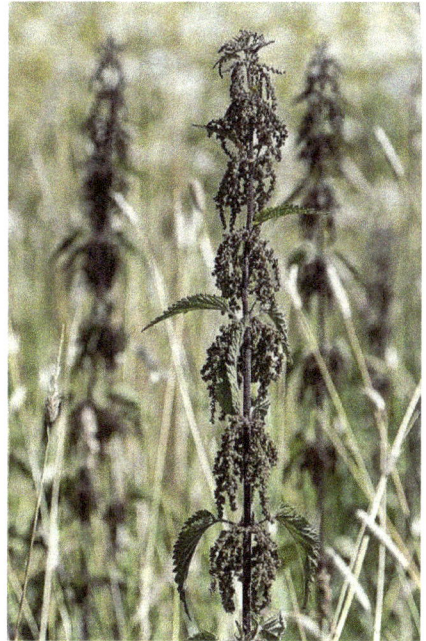

Nettles.[16]

- **Preferred Habitats:** Nettles prefer moist, fertile soils and are commonly found along stream banks and in pastures and abandoned agricultural land.

- **Seasonal Nuances:** Nettle leaves should be harvested as early as possible, as they grow progressively tougher and stringer – especially after flowering, which generally begins in May and lasts until early fall. Take great care when harvesting, as the stinging hairs are present even in very young plants, and wear gloves when handling plant materials.

- **Nutritional Benefits:** Nettles are a great source of vitamins A, C, and K. They also contain iron, calcium, and magnesium.

- **Identification Tips:** Look for the coarsely toothed leaves (they look a little like mint leaves) and use a magnifier to locate the stinging hairs. Also look for the plants' square, reddish stems and inconspicuous white or green flowers.

- **Potential Lookalikes/Poisonous Counterparts:** False nettle (*Boehmeria cylindriaca*) resembles stinging nettle and grows in similar habitats, but its leaves lack stinging hairs. It isn't poisonous, but it's not commonly eaten (except by mistake).

Chickweed

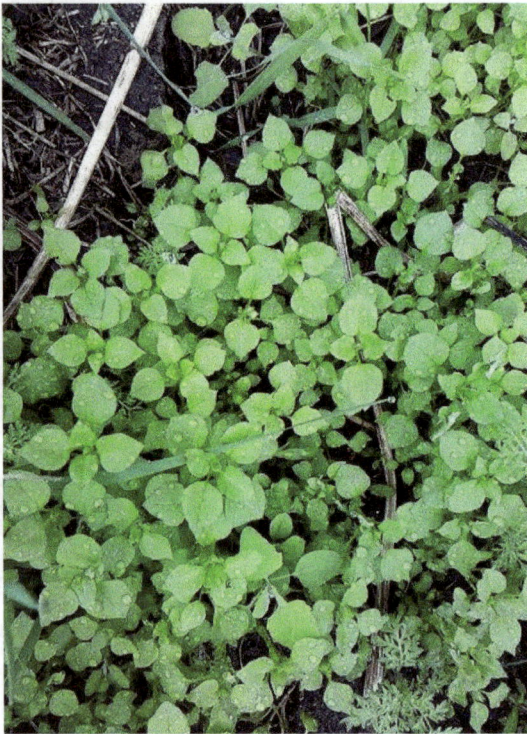

Chickweed.[17]

- **Distinct Characteristics:** Chickweed (*Stellaria media*) is a low-growing annual, often one of the first plants to emerge early spring. Its creeping stems are vaguely squarish and have a distinctive line of hairs running down one side only. It has small, teardrop-shaped leaves that are oppositely arranged on the stem. The white flowers, which emerge from leaf axils, are about as big around as a pencil eraser and have five deeply notched petals that might look like ten at first glance.

- **Preferred Habitats:** Chickweed, like many annual weeds, does best in fertile soils with plenty of water and sunlight. It can often be found in low places where water collects, especially human-made habitats like lawns, drainage ditches, or swales.

- **Seasonal Nuances:** Chickweed usually emerges very early in the spring – in milder climates it often germinates in the fall and overwinters, to get a head start on the competition. It is generally most abundant in spring, with a second flush in autumn in some locations, and can be harvested any time it is available.

- **Nutritional Benefits:** Chickweed is a good source of vitamins A and C, and is surprisingly high in protein for a leafy green. Like a number of other leafy greens (spinach and kale, among others), chickweed also contains saponins, chemicals that can be mildly toxic in large quantities, but which are mostly removed during the cooking process.

- **Identification Tips:** Chickweed has small, spade-shaped leaves (like the suit of cards) that grow in opposed pairs along the stems, which have two distinctive traits: a line of short hairs along one side, and a threadlike "core" that you can see if you pull apart a stem.

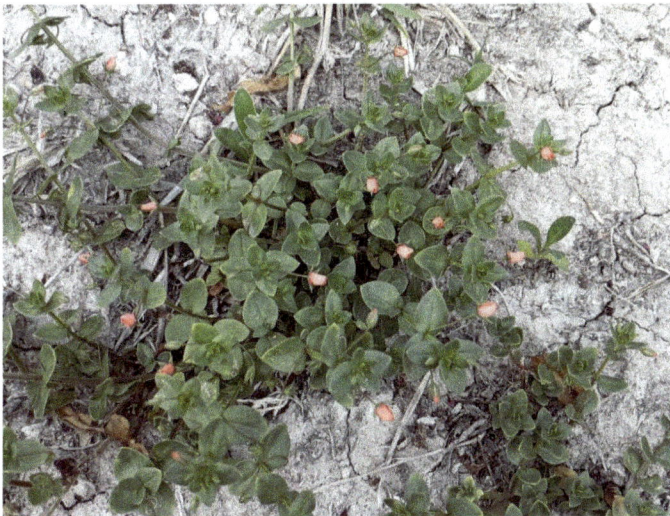

Scarlet pimpernel (*Anagallis arvensis*) is a toxic lookalike to chickweed: it has creeping stems, opposite leaves, and grows in similar habitats.[18]

- **Potential Lookalikes/Poisonous Counterparts:** Chickweed's appearance and growth habit are not especially distinctive without flowers, and can be easy for beginners to confuse with other creeping annuals, such as the toxic scarlet pimpernel *(Anagallis arvensis)*, which has a similar appearance and is often found in similar habitats. The easiest way to avoid confusion is to find the

Purslane (*Portulaca oleracea*)

Purslane (Portulaca oleracea).[19]

- **Distinct Characteristics:** Purslane **(*Portulaca oleracea*)** is a low-growing, succulent summer annual. Its fleshy, often reddish stems radiate from a central taproot and creep along the ground, forming large mats or clumps; its opposite, spoon-shaped leaves are barely half an inch long and, like the stems, distinctly fleshy. The small yellow flowers are five-petaled and often close in the afternoon to conserve water.

- **Preferred Habitats:** Purslane is a specialist of dry, disturbed soils, and is often seen growing luxuriantly from cracks in the pavement! As a native species, it can sometimes ve found in wilderness areas, but is much more common near human habitation.

- **Seasonal Nuances:** Purslane is at the peak of its growth and productivity in mid-to-late summer, typically from June through August. Try to harvest before the plant sets seed, as it begins to wither soon afterwards.

- **Nutritional Benefits:** Purslane is surprisingly rich in nutrients: vitamins A and C, potassium, magnesium, iron, and calcium. It's also a good source of omega-3 fatty acids.

- **Identification Tips:** Purslane's succulent leaves and stems are distinctive. The small yellow flowers have five notched petals and a cup-like shape when open.

Prostrate spurge (*Euphorbia maculata*) can be mistaken for purslane, but its stems bleed a milky white sap – often, though not always, the sign of a toxic plant.[20]

- **Potential Lookalikes/Poisonous Counterparts:** Prostrate spurge (*Euphorbia maculata*) is a common weedy annual that can appear similar to purslane due to its mat-forming growth habit and red stems. Like most spurges, it is toxic to humans, but is easily distinguished by its more fragile appearance (it's not succulent like purslane) and the milky white sap it exudes from broken stems or leaves.

Goosefoot (Chenopodium album)

Goosefoot (*Chenopodium album*)[21]

- **Distinct Characteristics:** Goosefoot (*Chenopodium album*) is an annual herb with lance-or diamond-shaped leaves, two to three inches long and a little more than half as wide, which look a little like a goose's foot. The leaves, especially the upper (younger) ones, are often covered in fine hairs that look like white powder. The flowers are inconspicuous and wind-pollinated, growing in clusters at the ends of the stems.

- **Preferred Habitats:** Goosefoot will grow nearly anywhere, but is most abundant on fertile, disturbed soils, from roadsides and vacant lots to farms and construction sites.

- **Seasonal Nuances:** Goosefoot leaves can be harvested throughout the spring and early summer. They are tender and fleshy when young, with a flavor and texture similar to spinach, but become stringy as they age, so only harvest the youngest leaves. In summer, the flower buds can be cooked and eaten whole like broccoli, while the seeds can be harvested in fall and eaten like quinoa (which is closely related).

- **Nutritional Benefits:** Goosefoot is a great source of vitamins A, C, and K, and the leaves are surprisingly high in protein. The seeds are proten-packed too, but have to be hulled to remove the papery seed coat, which contains bitter saponins.

- **Identification Tips:** The large size and sprawling growth habit of goosefoot is likely the first thing that will catch your eye. Look closer and you should notice the leaves, lance-shaped near the top of the plant and more diamond-shaped below, as well as the powdery coating on the upper leaves. The stems often develop reddish veins, and may turn entirely red in very sunny environments.

Ivyleaf groundcherry (*Physalis hederifolia*) is common in the West, and can sometimes appear similar to goosefoot. Its fruits are edible if cooked, but the leaves are toxic.[22]

- **Potential Lookalikes/Poisonous Counterparts:** Pitseed goosefoot (*Chenopodium berlandieri*) is a native species closely related to common goosefoot, and so similar as to be indistinguishable. It is also edible, and the two can be used interchangeably. Young goosefoot plants may resemble some nightshade species like groundcherry (*Physalis* spp.), but nightshade leaves are smooth, not toothed, and do not have the "powdery" appearance of goosefoot; they also produce true flowers with five petals, while goosefoot's flowers lack petals and are inconspicuous.

Miner's Lettuce (*Claytonia perfoliata*)

Miner's lettuce (*Claytonia perfoliata*).[28]

- **Distinct Characteristics:** Miner's lettuce (*Claytonia perfoliata*) is a low-growing, succulent annual that starts growing as early as December or January, and is gone by the start of summer. Its leaves come in two varieties: first, a rosette of rounded, spoon-shaped leaves with very long **petioles** (leaf stalks), and later unusual clasping **cauline** or stem leaves that grow all the way around the stem. The small white or pink flowers emerge in mid-to-late spring.

- **Preferred Habitats:** Miner's lettuce likes shade, and is commonly found in woodland edges, stream banks, and recently burned chaparral or sagebrush communities.

- **Seasonal Nuances:** The peak of growth for miner's lettuce is late winter, when soaking rains allow it to survive in environments that will be bone-dry later in the year. This is the best time to harvest it, too, as plants acquire a sour flavor after flowering.

- **Nutritional Benefits:** Miner's lettuce is rich in vitamins A, C, and B-complex, as well as calcium, iron, and phosphorus.

- **Identification Tips:** The rounded leaves grow in a rosette formation close to the ground, and are a bit reminiscent of purslane (*Portulaca oleracea*), a related species. The stalks or petioles are very long, and later in the year become tinged with red at their bases.

- **Potential Lookalikes/Poisonous Counterparts:** The succulent leaves of miner's lettuce – both rosette and cauline leaves – appear well before most other plants, and are so unusual in appearance as to be unmistakable. The related pink purslane (*Claytonia sibirica*) is somewhat similar, but lacks the unusual stem leaves and has all pink flowers. It is also edible, though its flavor is not as good as miner's lettuce.

Watercress (Nasturtium officinale)

Watercress (*Nasturtium officinale*).[34]

- **Distinct Characteristics:** Watercress (*Nasturtium officinale*) is a semi-aquatic, perennial herb with hollow stems that can reach up to three feet long or longer and float on the surface of moving water. The leaves are compound, with 3, 5, 7, or 9 leaflets and a total length of two to five inches. The small, four-petaled white flowers grow in clusters from the top of the plant.

- **Preferred Habitats:** Watercress is always found near water, most often on the banks of rivers, ponds, or lakes where it grows partially submerged in the shallows. Less commonly, it can be found at the edges of seeps and springs where groundwater emerges from bedrock, providing a perennial source of water.

- **Seasonal Nuances:** Watercress grows more or less year-round depending on the climate, and in many places can be found throughout the winter. It can be harvested at any time of year, but sometimes becomes bitter after flowering in summer.

- **Nutritional Benefits:** Watercress is rich in vitamins A, C, and K.

- **Identification Tips:** Watercress is in the same family as musard and cabbage (Brassicaceae), but unlike these plants it has compound leaves. The stems are even more unusual, and quite distinctive: they are hollow, allowing them to float on the surface of the water. The cross-shaped white flowers are more typical of other plants in the family, as is the peppery flavor.

- **Potential Lookalikes/Poisonous Counterparts:** A number of plants in the mustard family have similar leaves, especially pepperweeds (*Lepidium*). While all plants in the cabbage family are edible, most prefer drier habitats and none have the hollow stems of watercress.

Wild Mustard (*Brassica nigra*)

Wild mustard (*Brassica nigra*)[25]

- **Distinct Characteristics:** Wild mustard (*Brassica nigra*), also known as black mustard, is a common weedy relative of cultivated cabbage (*Brassica oleracea*). Its lower leaves, which can reach up to a foot long, are sparsely hairy, quite variable in shape but generally widest near the middle and deeply lobed (sometimes so deeply as to appear compound). The stem leaves are similar in shape but generally smaller. The flowers emerge from the tips of the stems, which are often much branched; they are yellow, four-petaled, and cross-shaped, similar to many plants in the cabbage family. The fruits, slender seed pods called **siliques**, look a little like beans, but point straight up instead of hanging down.

- **Preferred Habitats:** Wild mustard grows profusely in disturbed habitats such as old pastures, recently burned areas, and even vacant lots. In some parts of the West it has become highly invasive, so this is one plant where the rule of sustainable harvest doesn't apply!

- **Seasonal Nuances:** The leaves of wild mustard are best before the plant flowers in late spring, and smaller leaves generally have a better texture. The seed ripens in the fall, and can be harvested throughout the fall and winter.

- **Nutritional Benefits:** Wild mustard greens are high in vitamins A, C, and K. Like most species in the cabbage family, they are also rich in glucosinolates, complex compounds that give the greens their peppery taste.

- **Identification Tips:** The basal leaves of wild mustard are petiolate (have visible stalks) and can grow to be nearly a foot long; the upper surfaces of older leaves are often bristly or hairy. The stems often branch profusely at the tips, and -- unlike most common lookalikes -- the cauline leaves do not clasp the stem.

- **Potential Lookalikes/Poisonous Counterparts:** Wild mustard's only real lookalikes are all related species in the cabbage family: field mustard (*Brassica rapa*) and brown mustard (*Brassica juncea*) are most common in the West. The former has clasping leaves; the latter produces flowering branches up and down the stem, rather than just at the top.

Nodding Onion (*Allium cernuum*)

Nodding onion (*Allium cernuum*)[26]

- **Distinct Characteristics:** Nodding onion (*Allium cernuum*) is a perennial plant in the lily family, with long, narrow leaves and distinctive nodding flower stalks topped by small pink or white flowers. The whole plant has a strong garlicky or onion smell that is quite distinctive.

- **Preferred Habitats:** Nodding onion prefers moist soils but are otherwise widely distributed, most common in open woods and stream banks.

- **Seasonal Nuances:** Nodding onion greens can be harvested at any time of year; bulbs are best harvested from large and established plants, in the fall before the tops die back.

- **Nutritional Benefits:** Wild onions are high in vitamins A, C, and B-complex.

- **Identification Tips:** As its name suggests, the drooping or nodding flowers are distinctive; prior to flowering, the plants are best identified by smell

Potential Lookalikes/Poisonous Counterparts: Many species of *Allium* look like nodding onion; any species with a strong garlic/onion smell is edible. Nodding onion can be easily distinguished by its nodding flowers, when these are available. Some toxic species in the lily family have foliage that may appear similar to beginning foragers; the best way to avoid these is simply to avoid any plants without a strong garlic/onion smell!

Flowers

Nasturtiums

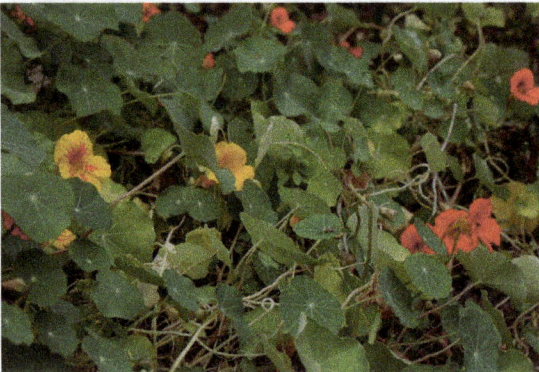

Nasturtiums.[27]

- **Distinct Characteristics:** Nasturtium (*Tropaeolum majus*) is a trailing or vine-like annual with large, round leaves and funnel-shaped flowers that come in yellow, orange, red, and pink.

- **Preferred Habitats:** Nasturtiums prefer moist soils but grow well in lean, more difficult environments. They will happily colonize disturbed areas, such as gardens, the edges of pathways, and trails, though they persist only in mild climates.

- **Seasonal Nuances:** Nasturtiums emerge after the last frost and bloom in mid-summer, dying back in late autumn. Both the leaves and flowers are edible at any time of year, but young leaves are best, and plants grown in sunnier or warmer locations tend to have a spicier flavor.

- **Nutritional Benefits:** Nasturtiums contain glucosinolates, a compound believed to have anti-cancer effects.

- **Identification Tips:** Nasturtium leaves are glossy, waxy, and green, with lighter veins and a pale dot in the center. Their flowers look a bit like petunias or violets, with five asymmetrical petals: two above, three below. The entire plant also has a strong, mustardy scent.

- **Potential Lookalikes/Poisonous Counterparts:** Water pennywort (*Hydrocotyle* spp.) has leaves that can appear almost identical to nasturtium leaves, but the plant produces white, spherical clusters of flowers instead of large single blooms. Water pennywort is also rarely found away from standing water, so it doesn't often share habitat with nasturtiums.

Violets

Violets.[38]

- **Distinct Characteristics:** Violets are low-growing, perennial herbs with heart-shaped leaves and five-petaled flowers in shades of purple, blue, white, and yellow. The flowers are typically around one inch in diameter, and the plants have a low, spreading growth pattern, only reaching 6-12 inches tall.

- **Preferred Habitats:** Violets prefer dewy environments with shade. This includes forested understories, woodland edges, and along the edges of streams.

- **Seasonal Nuances:** Violets are cool-weather plants whose flowers overflow in spring and early summer. However, as temperatures warm up, the plant goes dormant until the next growing season.

- **Nutritional Benefits:** Violets contain a good amount of antioxidants, particularly anthocyanins. While not the most mineral-dense flower, they do contain traces of calcium, iron, and even a little protein.

- **Identification Tips:** Violets grow low to the ground, usually less than a foot tall. The heart-shaped leaves are dark green and glossy, often with very long stalks or petioles. The flowers are distinctive, with two petals above and three below; they range from nearly white to deep purple.

- **Potential Lookalikes/Poisonous Counterparts:** While violets in bloom are practically unmistakable, their leaves can be confused with a few other species, including ground ivy, garlic mustard, and lesser celandine. The leaves of ground ivy and garlic mustard are strongly scented (ground ivy smells like camphor, garlic mustard smells like garlic) and both are edible. Lesser celandine is toxic when eaten raw, and can be difficult to distinguish from violets before its bright yellow flowers emerge, so when in doubt, wait for flowers.

Pansies

Pansies.[29]

- **Distinct Characteristics:** Pansies are low-growing, herbaceous plants that reach six to 12 inches in height. Their most famous feature is their multi-petaled flowers. Each pansy bloom has five fused petals, creating a slightly ruffled, face-like appearance. The petals have a spectrum of solid shades, including purple, blue, yellow, and white, and even bicolor and tricolor combinations of these colors.

- **Preferred Habitats:** Pansies like well-draining, nutrient-rich soils that are slightly acidic. The area must be cool and damp, or they will struggle and start to wither.

- **Seasonal Nuances:** As cool-weather plants, pansies enjoy the milder seasons of spring and fall because they can direct their energy into producing many of their multi-petaled flowers. Exposure to hot, dry weather in the summer causes a decline in the number of flowers they produce, and the existing ones will wilt or look discolored.

- **Nutritional Benefits:** Pansies contain small amounts of iron, calcium, and magnesium, but they are very high in vitamins C and A.

- **Identification Tips:** Pansies are quite easy to identify, even for those new to plant recognition. Like violets (technically they *are* violets), they have flowers with five petals – two above, three below – that are joined at the base and almost flat in cross-section.

- **Potential Lookalikes/Poisonous Counterparts:** You are unlikely to mistake pansies for any other plant, though less showy plants may appear similar to violets.

Dandelion Flowers

Dandelion flower.[80]

- **Distinct Characteristics:** Like all plants in the sunflower family (Asteraceae), dandelion "flowers" are composed of dozens of individual yellow florets. Unlike daisies and sunflowers, dandelions have no disk florets at their centers, but consist solely of ray florets.

- **Preferred Habitats:** Dandelions are some of the most resilient and adaptable plants in existence. Although they grow best in moist, fertile soils, they routinely colonize poor or dry soils as well. They are closely associated with humans, however, and are generally found growing abundantly in or near human-modified habitats.

- **Seasonal Nuances:** Dandelion flowers bloom nearly year-round, limited only by rainfall and warm temperatures. However, they are most prolific in spring, and their flowers last longer than in the heat of summer.

- **Nutritional Benefits:** Dandelion flowers contain diuretic compounds, fiber, prebiotics, vitamin A, and vitamin C.

- **Identification Tips:** The bright yellow blooms of dandelions may be eye-catching, but make sure to examine the plants closely: if they're true dandelions, their leaves will be deeply lobed and arranged in a rosette, with a single flowering stalk in the middle. The stalks of dandelions are hollow, unbranched – one stalk, one flower – and bleed a white, milky sap when broken.

- **Potential Lookalikes/Poisonous Counterparts:** Although no toxic plants resemble dandelions, it's easy to confuse them with many closely related plants in the sunflower family like hawkweed, cat's paw, and chicory. Rather than try to learn dozens of possible lookalikes, just remember that true dandelions – and *only* dandelions – have hollow flowering stalks that don't branch.

Sunflowers

Sunflowers (*Helianthus annus*)[31]

- **Distinct Characteristics:** Sunflowers (*Helianthus annuus*) are large, annual plants with composite flowers 2-3 inches in diameter. The flowers consist of a central disc surrounded by vivid yellow "petals" that are actually individual flowers.

- **Preferred Habitats:** Sunflowers are disturbance-adapted species, and often *irruptive*, meaning that they may be extraordinarily abundant in a location one year, but produce few or no plants the following year.

- **Seasonal Nuances:** Sunflowers emerge in late spring and bloom in summer, producing seeds that ripen in the late summer or early autumn. As the seeds ripen, the plants wither and die from the ground up.

- **Nutritional Benefits:** Sunflowers have concentrated amounts of vitamin E and the mineral selenium.

- **Identification Tips:** The bright green stems are often quite hairy, as are the heart-shaped leaves. As the inflorescence begins to develop, look for the green petal-like bracts that surround the bud. Once the plant blooms, there's no mistaking the giant blooms.

- **Potential Lookalikes/Poisonous Counterparts:** Many plants in the sunflower family have inflorescences that look like sunflowers, but they are nearly always much smaller, and most have yellow or green centers instead of the sunflower's brown disc. No species in the family is known to be toxic.

Wild Rose (*Rosa woodsii*)

Wild rose (*Rosa woodsii*)[32]

- **Distinct Characteristics:** Wild roses (*Rosa woodsii*) are bushy perennials with prickly stems and large, five-petaled pink flowers. The compound leaves have five or seven leaflets, each sharply serrated and about an inch long.

- **Preferred Habitats:** Wild roses are extremely adaptable and found across the region, growing in prairies and open woodlands, roadsides and pastures, and even in the understory of mountain forests.

- **Seasonal Nuances:** Wild roses generally bloom in late spring or early summer, and the hips ripen in late summer or autumn.

- **Nutritional Benefits:** Wild roses are exceptionally high in vitamin C, beneficial omega-3 and omega-6 fatty acids, and small amounts of B vitamins, copper, and manganese.

- **Identification Tips:** Wild rose plants have compound leaves, meaning each leaf comprises several smaller leaflets arranged in a pinnate pattern along the stem. The leaflets should be oval or oblong, with serrated edges. The flower should have five petals with a cluster of yellow stamens in the center like a pincushion.

- **Potential Lookalikes/Poisonous Counterparts:** Wild roses have few lookalikes, especially in bloom. The only plants that look remotely similar to wild roses are brambles (like blackberries and raspberries), which also have prickly stems and big, five-petaled flowers. However, they are generally smaller than wild rose blooms and develop into berries instead of hips. One "impostor" to watch out for is the multiflora rose (*Rosa multiflora*): it's a true rose, but it's an exotic species that has become seriously invasive, forming impenetrable thickets and choking out native plants wherever it goes.

Blue Elder (*Sambucus cerulea*)

Blue Elder (*Sambucus cerulea*).[33]

- **Distinct Characteristics:** Blue elder (*Sambucus cerulea*) is a shrub or small tree with opposite, compound leaves, each with 5, 7, or 9 serrated leaflets. Like the closely related European elder (*Sambucus nigra*), blue elder is easily identified in spring by its showy white flowers, which are borne in large, flat-topped clusters and ripen into sky-blue berries in the summer or early fall.

- **Preferred Habitats:** Elders are early-successional species in many forest ecosystems in the West, meaning that they grow abundantly in forest openings and recently disturbed areas. They are commonly found along streams, too, often in association with quaking aspen (*Populus tremuloides*).

- **Seasonal Nuances:** In the Mountain West, blue elder blooms from late May through July. The berries are best harvested at summer's end, usually mid-August or early September.

- **Nutritional Benefits:** Elderflowers are rich in vitamins A and C, as well as antioxidants and flavonoids that can improve immune system function. However, flowers and berries both should be thoroughly cooked before consumption, as they can be toxic when eaten raw in large quantities.

- **Identification Tips:** The leaves of blue elder are both compound and oppositely arranged, and the leaflets have serrated margins – this is a fairly rare combination of traits and can help identify the plant. The flower clusters of the elder are branching and flat-topped, the branching stalks often turning red as the fruits develop. The berries appear light blue due to a powdery coating that can be rubbed off to reveal a glossy purple or black beneath.

Water hemlock.[a]

- **Potential Lookalikes/Poisonous Counterparts:** Black or European elder *(Sambucus nigra)* is less common in the west than blue elder, but the two species are closely related and used in the same ways. The best way to recognize black elder is the black berries! Water hemlocks (*Cicuta* spp.) are highly toxic plants that also grow near water, and are superficially quite similar to blue elder, down to the compound leaves and white flowers. Despite appearances, though, they aren't at all closely related; the leaves of water hemlock are alternate, not opposite, and the plants are not woody, dying back to the ground each winter.

Chives

Chives.[35]

- **Distinct Characteristics:** Chives (*Allium schoenoprasum*) are closely related to wild onions, and have long, narrow leaves that may reach well over a foot in length. The flowers are a distinctive pale purple or pink in color, and are borne in spiky, pom-pom-like clusters.

- **Preferred Habitats:** Chives grow in cool, moist environments, often on thin and rocky soils. In the wild, they are often found along gravelly stream banks or even sprouting directly from bedrock. However, they have also frequently escaped cultivation in farms or gardens and thus are often found far outside their normal habitats.

- **Seasonal Nuances:** Chives can be harvested from spring to early autumn, when the plants die back to the ground.

- **Nutritional Benefits:** Chives are a rich source of antioxidants and contain vitamins A, C, and K.

- **Identification Tips:** The leaves of chives are narrower and rounder than most related species, and clasp the flowering stalks as they emerge. The pink inflorescences are quite distinctive, both for their color and their spiky shape: most wild onions *(Allium* spp.) have looser and more open flower heads.

- **Potential Lookalikes/Poisonous Counterparts:** Wild onions can appear similar to chives, both in appearance and smell; they can be distinguished by their leaves, which are flatter and (slightly) broader, as well as their flowers, which form open clusters rather than the compact "puffs" produced by chives.

Fireweed (*Chamaenerion angustifolium*)

Fireweed (*Chamaenerion angustifolium*).[36]

- **Distinct Characteristics:** Fireweed (*Chamaenerion angustifolium*) is named for its tendency to rapidly colonize disturbed areas, especially after a wildfire. It is an unmistakable plant, growing up to six feet tall or taller, with distinctive lance-shaped leaves. Huge, lilac-like spikes of magenta emerge in late summer, blooming from the bottom up. The flowers mature into long, thin seed pods that split open in the fall, releasing hundreds of downy seeds that float on the wind for miles.

- **Preferred Habitats:** You'll find fireweed growing in open, disturbed areas – places that have recently been logged, burned, or otherwise cleared. It loves the nutrient-rich, well-draining soils of mountain meadows, forest edges, and stream banks.

- **Seasonal Nuances:** Fireweed flowers from mid-summer through early fall. The flowers ripen into long, thin fruits, which peel open when ripe to release hundreds of seeds, each with a tuft of long hairs at one end that acts as a "parachute" to aid dispersal by autumn winds.

- **Nutritional Benefits:** The young shoots, leaves, and flowers are all edible and high in vitamin A, vitamin C, calcium, and iron. The mature leaves can be lightly fermented to make a tea similar to black tea, known in Russia as Ivan Chai.

- **Identification Tips:** Fireweed impresses first by its sheer numbers, then by the size of individual plants. The willow-like leaves, four to six inches long when fully grown, have a distinctive circular venation: the lateral veins merge into a single vein that runs all the way around the edge of the leaf. The bright pink flowers, which bloom from the bottom of the plant to the top, are zygomorphic (bilaterally symmetrical) and have long, whisker-like stamens. The seed pods are

- **Potential Lookalikes/Poisonous Counterparts:** From a distance, the invasive purple loosestrife *(Lythrum salicaria)* looks a bit like fireweed, with lance-like leaves and profuse magenta flowers. However, closer inspection will reveal the numerous distinctions: purple loosestrife has branching stems, while fireweed generally has a compact, almost Christmas tree-like shape; the leaves of purple loosestrife are opposite, while those of fireweed are spirally alternate. Finally, its flowers are much smaller than fireweed's, six-petaled, and actinomorphic (radially symmetrical). It is not known to be toxic, and in fact has been used in European herbal medicine for centuries.

Wild Berries

Wild Strawberry (*Fragaria vesca* and *F. virginica*)

Wild strawberries (*Fragaria vesca*).[87]

- **Distinct Characteristics:** Wild strawberries (*Fragaria* spp.), like their cousins blackberries and raspberries (*Rubus* spp.), are rambling perennials in the rose family, with a growth habit somewhere between a vine and an herb. Though individual plants rarely rise above ten or twelve inches in height, they cover a lot of ground via runners or **stolons**, much like the grass in your lawn (if you have one). Their bright green, serrated leaves are trifoliate (with three lobes or leaflets) and look a bit like blackberry leaves, as do their white, five-petaled flowers. The berries, which ripen in mid-summer, are unmistakable and unmissable.

- **Preferred Habitats:** Wild strawberries will tolerate a wide range of conditions, but are basically woodland plants, with a particular fondness for disturbed areas like edges and clearings. Roadsides and the edges of hiking trails are also likely places. One thing to keep in mind is that wild strawberries will often persist in very shady environments without ever producing fruits -- so don't assume that you've found a strawberry patch just because you've found strawberry *plants*.

- **Seasonal Nuances:** Wild strawberries are generally ready to harvest by July, though northern or high-altitude foragers may have to wait until August. The hardest part isn't finding ripe berries, though – it's competing with all the other wildlife! Remember to take only a few berries from each plant, to ensure that the rest of the forest can benefit from them.

- **Nutritional Benefits:** Wild strawberries have a high concentration of vitamin C, manganese, and iron.

- **Identification Tips:** You probably don't need help identifying a strawberry, but the plants can be somewhat inconspicuous before they bloom. Look for the distinctive trifoliate leaves, then look closer: you should be able to find stolons connecting the plants to one another. The flowers are small, a little over half an inch wide, but quite beautiful, with five crisp white (very rarely pink) petals and numerous conspicuous stamens at the center.

Mock strawberry.[38]

- **Potential Lookalikes/Poisonous Counterparts:** Mock strawberries (*Potentilla indica*) have serrated, three-lobed leaves and can appear remarkably similar to wild strawberries, albeit much smaller – right down to the pea-sized fruits These are preceded, however, by yellow flowers instead of white, indicating that these plants are more closely related to cinquefoils (*Potentilla reptans*) than true strawberries. The fruits are perfectly edible, by the way, although they have almost no flavor.

Serviceberry (*Amelanchier alnifolia* and *A. utahensis*)

Serviceberries (*Amelanchier alnifolia*)[39]

- **Distinct Characteristics:** Serviceberries are shrubs in the genus *Amelanchier*, of which the Saskatoon serviceberry (*A. alnifolia*) -- often simply called "saskatoon" – is the most common in the West. Serviceberries are profusely multi-trunked, with dozens of stems arising from a single rootstock.. The leaves are oval-shaped to nearly circular, with prominent pinnate veins and serrated margins, resemble alder (*Alnus* spp.) leaves. Large clusters of white flowers appear in late spring or early summer, developing into small, dark blue "berries" (technically they're more like apples) in July and August.

- **Preferred Habitats:** Serviceberries are commonly found in low elevation pine forests, where the canopy is relatively sparse, as well as along mountain streams and creeks. It can thrive on infertile soil, but grows best in full sun and near a consistent water source;

- **Seasonal Nuances:** Serviceberry trees and shrubs bloom in the late spring, but the berries are ripe and ready for harvesting in mid-to-late summer.

- **Nutritional Benefits:** Serviceberries are an amazing source of vitamin C. They also contain dietary fiber, about 7 grams per cup.

- **Identification Tips:** Serviceberries are easy to identify when flowers or fruits are present; prior to flowering, they're best identified by their round leaves, which contrast strongly with the reddish or light-brown stems and are often only partially serrated, along the furthest edge of the leaf.

- **Potential Lookalikes/Poisonous Counterparts:** Serviceberries can sometimes be confused with chokecherries, which also have white flowers and edible berries. Chokecherry flowers are smaller, and arranged in compact hanging clusters; their leaves are larger and more oblong, with pointed instead of rounded tips. Their fruits are glossy, while serviceberries are duller, resembling blueberries.

Huckleberries (*Vaccinium scoparium*)

Huckleberries (*Vaccinium scoparium*).[40]

- **Distinct Characteristics:** Huckleberries (*Vaccinium* spp.) are closely related to cranberries (*Vaccinium* subg. *oxycoccum*) and blueberries (*Vaccinium* subg. *cyanococcus*), and over a dozen species can be found in the West. Mountain huckleberry (*V.*

scoparium) is one of the most common and easy to recognize species, with distinctive angled twigs and finely serrated, paper-thin leaves. The delicate white and pink flowers mature into dark purple berries that look a lot like glossy blueberries.

- **Preferred Habitats:** Huckleberries, like many other species of *Vaccinium,* are specialists of disturbed habitats, spreading rapidly via rhizomes (underground stems) to colonize openings. They are often a dominant understory species in recently burned or logged coniferous forests and rocky slopes, especially above and adjacent to streams.

- **Seasonal Nuances:** Huckleberries bloom relatively late in the season – generally May or early June – and the berries ripen in late summer. Depending on latitude and elevation, that might be as early as July (lower) or as late as the end of August (higher).

- **Nutritional Benefits:** Huckleberry is a superfood, containing an impressive amount of vitamins, minerals, fiber, antioxidants, and polyphenols.

- **Identification Tips:** Mountain huckleberries are spreading shrubs, generally about waist-high but often forming dense clonal colonies. Apart from the berries themselves, the leaves may be the most distinctive part of the plants. They're about an inch long, quite thin (the specific epithet *membranaceum* refers to their membrane-like texture), and finely serrated; look closer (you might need a hand lens) and you'll see a tiny hair at the apex of each tooth. The white, cream, or pink bell-shaped flowers emerge in clusters from the leaf axils, and are rarely more than half a centimeter in diameter; the fruits look remarkably like glossy blueberries, with a color ranging from deep red (wait a while) to nearly black (good to go!).

- **Potential Lookalikes/Poisonous Counterparts:** Huckleberries have few lookalikes outside their genus – but as noted above, mountain huckleberries are far from the only species of huckleberry in the West, and in many places other species may be more abundant locally. The diminutive littleleaf huckleberry (*V. scoparium*) and dwarf bilberry (*V. caespitosum*) are two of the more frequently encountered species in the interior West. It's a good idea to learn the most common species in your particular area, as they're all edible and well worth harvesting.

Raspberries

Raspberries.[41]

- **Distinct Characteristics:** Wild raspberries (Rubus strigosus), like other brambles (*Rubus* spp.), are distinctive plants at any time of year: if the bright red berries don't catch your eye, the prickly stems will certainly catch your pant leg! Raspberries stand out from other brambles mainly by their stems or canes, which are armed not only with prickles but bristly hairs as well – as well as their small white flowers, which emerge in clusters rather than individually.

- **Preferred Habitats:** The biggest and sweetest raspberries come from plants in moist habitats that get plenty of sunlight: sunny stream banks, roadsides, and recently burned forests often abound with raspberries. They're also commonly found "on the edge," whether that's a streambank or roadside -- even the side of a hiking trail!

- **Seasonal Nuances:** Like most of the other species in their genus, raspberries have perennial roots and biennial stems: each prickly cane spends the first year growing and the second year blooming and fruiting. Flowers emerge in late spring, and the berries ripen from mid-summer through early fall, depending on elevation and latitude. Higher-altitude (and northern) plants fruit later than their lower-altitude (and southern) cousins.

- **Nutritional Benefits:** Raspberries have high levels of vitamins C and K and manganese. They also contain healthy amounts of the phytochemical *ellagic acid.*

- **Identification Tips:** The stems of raspberry plants are not only prickly but often hairy as well, especially on new growth. They are also distinctively **pruinose**, meaning they have a pale bluish-gray coating like plums have. The leaves, which are 3- or 5-compound, have serrated margins and are often covered in the same bristly hairs as the stems. The fruits are greenish at first, and ripen into their distinctive deep red color. If you're not sure whether a berry is ripe, give it a gentle tug: if it doesn't release easily from the plant, you're probably too early.

- **Potential Lookalikes/Poisonous Counterparts:** Raspberries have no toxic lookalikes: any berry that looks like a raspberry (or blackberry) is edible, so don't fret too much over identification. That said, the hairy, pruinose stems of raspberry plants are distinctive enough to avoid confusion with other species. Thimbleberries and Rocky Mountain raspberries are most similar in appearance to raspberries, but their leaves are simple instead of compound and often much larger than raspberry leaves.

Blackberries (*Rubus* spp.)

Blackberries.[43]

- **Distinct Characteristics:** Blackberries aren't really a single species: they're brambles (*Rubus* spp.) with, well, black berries! In the West, the most common native brambles all have red fruits, so if you see a plant with dark colored fruits, it's very likely an exotic species: the most common are Himalayan blackberry (*R. armeniacus*) and European blackberry (*R. bifrons*) – which some botanists think is actually a single species.

- **Preferred Habitats:** Like most brambles, Himalayan blackberries love disturbed ground – so much, in fact, that they've become invasive throughout much of the West Coast, where they form huge thickets. They're especially common in pine woodlands with open canopies, and can colonize burned or logged forest with amazing speed.

- **Seasonal Nuances:** In the West, nearly all brambles bloom in spring and set fruit throughout the summer. Himalayan blackberries stagger their flowering and fruiting times, and at least some plants will have ripe fruits from April all the way to September.

- **Nutritional Benefits:** Blackberries are a known source of vitamins C and K, manganese, and fiber. The dark pigments that give the berries their intense color contain anthocyanins, a powerful antioxidant.

- **Identification Tips:** Himalayan blackberries have a similar growth habit to native species, but supercharged: these plants can easily reach ten feet high, or sprawl along the ground for twenty feet or more! The stems are often hexagonal in cross-section, and their prickles are hooked. The leaves are compound and distinctively palmate, meaning all the leaflets (usually 5) sprout from a single point. The flowers are small – about a half inch in diameter – but they make up for their size in sheer numbers, emerging by the dozens in long clusters.

- **Potential Lookalikes/Poisonous Counterparts:** Despite the fact that as many as a hundred species of bramble can be found in North America, you're really not likely to confuse any of them with Himalayan blackberry: apart from its distinctive hooked prickles and palmate leaves, no other species grows as vigorously or as large as Himalayan blackberries. Unfortunately, this is often at the expense of native ecosystems, but the good news is that this means there's no need to hold back when harvesting: you'll actually be doing the forest a favor!

Alpine Currant (*Ribes montigenum*)

Golden Currant *(Ribes aureum)*.[48]

- **Distinct Characteristics:** Currants and gooseberries (*Ribes* spp.) are low-growing shrubs with enormous diversity: over 50 species are found in North America alone, and distinguishing one from another isn't always easy. In the West, alpine currants (*R. montigenum*) are one of the most common edible species, and luckily they're quite distinctive, too: the stems are covered in spines and prickles, and the berries themselves often look to be just as heavily armed! In fact, they're perfectly safe to eat raw or cooked, with a tart but sweet flavor that is best showcased in jellies and pies.

- **Preferred Habitats:** Uplands and mountain forests are where the alpine currant makes its home, particularly dry spruce (Picea) and fir (*Abies*) forests. While it tolerates shade, it's a specialist of dry, rocky slopes and exposed sites, sometimes clinging on gamely in harsh alpine communities above the treeline.

- **Seasonal Nuances:** Alpine currants grow in places where there may only be 100 days per year above freezing. They bloom in late summer – much later than other species – and don't waste time, setting fruit as little as a month later. If you're in the mountains and it's warm enough to be outside, there's a good chance alpine currants will soon be ripe.

- **Nutritional Benefits:** For such unassuming little berries, currants are high in vitamin C, antioxidants, fiber, and even small amounts of beneficial minerals like potassium and manganese.

- **Identification Tips:** The leaves of alpine currant are 1-2 inches long and distinctively lobed, much like a geranium leaf. On new growth, you'll find a set of spines at the base of each leaf: anywhere from 1 to 5, generally 2 or 3. The flowers, which appear in the hundreds, are tiny – a quarter inch in diameter – and salmon-pink in color, with glandular hairs all over their outsides that contribute to the spicy aroma of the flowers. The fruits are glossy red berries about a centimeter in diameter, and are covered with the same hairs as the flowers.

- Potential Lookalikes/Poisonous Counterparts:

Chokecherries (*Prunus virginiana*)

Chokecherries."

- **Distinct Characteristics:** Chokecherries (*Prunus virginiana*) are closely related to peaches, plums, and cherries. Depending on how you look at them, they're either small trees or big shrubs, and like their orchard cousins, they have finely serrated leaves and smooth, glossy bark. However, their flowers – while similar in overall shape – are both smaller (about a half inch wide) and much more numerous, growing in large clusters rather than individually. The fruits look like small cherries, starting red and ripening to a glossy black. Even the ripe fruits have an astringent, puckery flavor that lends itself to processing or cooking.

- **Preferred Habitats:** Chokecherries are quite adaptable and can grow just about anywhere, from meadows to forests to foothills. They're often found along roadsides and fencerows, too.

- **Seasonal Nuances:** Chokecherries bloom later than peaches and true cherries, but the fruits develop faster, appearing in mid-summer and ripening by August or September. Only harvest ripe chokecherries, and don't eat them raw, as they contain toxins that are broken down by cooking or sun-drying them.

- **Nutritional Benefits:** The name "chokecherry" might make you think twice about eating it, but it is high in vitamin C, vitamin A, calcium, and iron. It also contains small amounts of cyanide-producing compounds, so maybe don't go overboard.

- **Identification Tips:** Chokecherries are easy to spot with their bundles of small, dark purple or black berries hanging in drooping bunches. The leaves are glossy green with toothed edges that turn shades of yellow, orange, and red in the fall. Like nearly all their closest relatives (which include peaches, plums, and almonds), the leaves of chokecherry smell like almond extract when crushed, with a distinctive bitter undertone.

- **Potential Lookalikes/Poisonous Counterparts:** There are plenty of species of *Prunus* in North America, but chokecherries are easily distinguished from close relatives by their long racemes of flowers – a rare trait in native species. You might mistake mountain ash (*Sorbus scopulina*) berries for unripe chokecherries, but the leaves of mountain ash are compound, while chokecherry leaves are simple. Chokecherries also darken as they ripen, while mountain ash berries remain bright red.

Nuts and Seeds

Pine Nuts, Pinyon (*Pinus edulis*)

Pine nuts.[46]

- **Distinct Characteristics:** Pine nuts are the edible seeds of certain pine tree species, of which the most common is the pinyon (*Pinus edulis*). Pinyons are smaller and stragglier than most pines – which makes them pretty easy to identify – and their cones are, too, rarely larger than a golf ball and with just five or ten overlapping scales. Inside each scale are two large brown seeds, which can be cracked open to reveal the cream-colored kernels within.

- **Preferred Habitats:** Pinyons are well-adapted to the dry, rocky slopes and mesas of the Mountain West. They're often found growing together with juniper (*Juniperus* spp.), and in fact the two trees are dominant across a huge swath of the Southwest. In Colorado, nearly a quarter of the total forested area is pinyon-juniper woodland.

- **Seasonal Nuances:** Pinyon cones appear in the summer and ripen in autumn, tumbling to the ground throughout the winter. Harvest the cones when they're fully brown but haven't opened yet: once they do, you'll be competing with pretty much every other animal in the area for the nuts, so don't wait for them to fall into your lap!

- **Nutritional Benefits:** Pine nuts are considered a superfood. They supply healthy fats, protein, fiber, vitamins, and minerals. Just a small handful pumps you full of vitamins B and E, magnesium, phosphorus, and the antioxidant *selenium*. Pine nuts also contain pinolenic acid, an essential fatty acid believed to suppress appetite.

- **Identification Tips:** Pinyon pines are small trees, often found growing alongside junipers. The needles always appear in bundled pairs and are relatively short – about two inches long. The cones are small (2 inches or less in diameter) and round, almost spherical; they have thick, woody scales that open slightly when the nuts ripen.

Potential Lookalikes/Poisonous Counterparts: You aren't likely to confuse a pine tree with anything else (except maybe a fir), and among pines, pinyons are both abundant and distinctive. With pine nuts, the hard part isn't finding the right species – it's finding a stick long enough to knock the cones down!

Hazelnuts (*Corylus cornuta*)

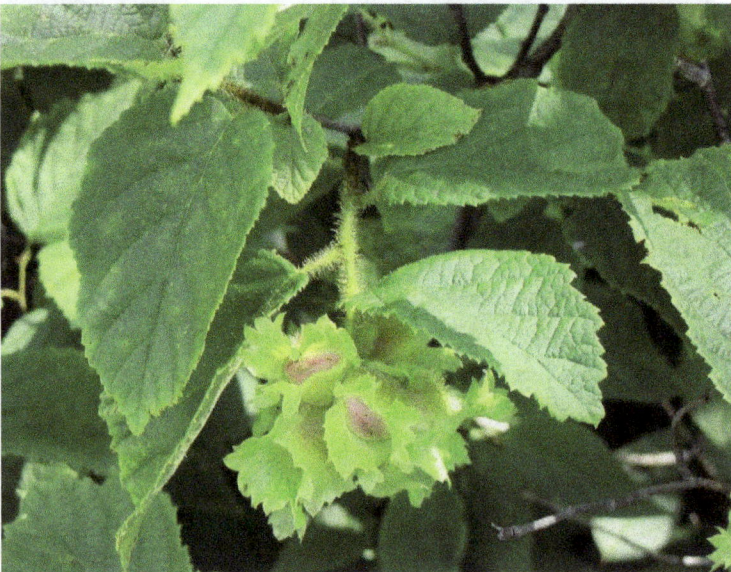

Hazelnuts.[46]

- **Distinct Characteristics:** Hazelnuts are the edible nuts produced by the hazel (*Corylus* spp.), a slender shrub or small tree with large, elm-like leaves and catkins of small flowers. The most common species in the West is the beaked hazel (*C. cornuta*), identifiable by its doubly serrated leaves, which are softly hairy on their undersides.

- **Preferred Habitats:** Hazels will not tolerate either full sun or deep shade, and grow best in woodlands or forests with an open canopy and understory. They can often be found growing along mountainous stream banks, open woodlands, and sometimes along fencerows and roadsides.

- **Seasonal Nuances:** Hazels bloom very early in spring, though their catkins (hanging clusters) of flowers are wind-pollinated and not very showy. The nuts ripen in autumn, and ripe nuts can be identified by their husks, which turn from green to brown. The husks are covered in small hairs that can irritate the skin of some people, so gloves should be worn when harvesting.

- **Nutritional Benefits:** Hazelnuts are a concentrated source of vitamin E, magnesium, phosphorus, and the antioxidant compound *copper.*

- **Identification Tips:** Hazel leaves are broad and somewhat leathery, with doubly toothed edges and a fuzzy texture underneath. The fruits are practically unmistakable, concealed in leaf-like husks with long "beaks" from which the species takes its name.

- **Potential Lookalikes/Poisonous Counterparts:** Chestnuts can resemble alder saplings because they have similar leaves and flowers, but alders generally grow much larger than chestnuts. The nuts themselves, with their bizarre enclosing bracts, are unmistakable. In northern California, the (even stranger-looking) beaked hazel is more common, and also produces edible nuts.

Pecans

Pecan.[47]

- **Distinct Characteristics:** Pecans are the oblong, thin-shelled nuts produced by (*Carya illinoensis*) pecan trees. They can grow over 100 feet tall, with sturdy trunks and spreading branches.

- **Preferred Habitats:** Pecans love the rich, well-draining soils of riparian areas and deep canyons. You'll see them lining the banks of rivers and streams or growing on the slopes of forested hillsides. They do best in areas that get plenty of sunlight and consistent moisture.

- **Seasonal Nuances:** Pecan trees flower in the spring, producing long, drooping catkins that eventually give way to the developing nuts. By late summer to early fall, the nuts will fully mature and be ready for harvesting.

- **Nutritional Benefits:** Pecans contain healthy fats, protein, fiber, and a good amount of vitamins and minerals. They're a trusted source of magnesium, zinc, and antioxidants like vitamin E.

- **Identification Tips:** It's hard to miss a pecan tree, considering they reach up to 100 feet. Its leaves are not just simple single leaves but a whole band of leaflets all growing off a single stem. The nuts are oblong and elongated, growing about one to two inches long. Each nut is enclosed in a tough, brown shell that splits open when ripe to reveal the nut, which is mottled black and brown. Put all these details together, and you know you're looking at a pecan.

- **Potential Lookalikes/Poisonous Counterparts:** There are a few species that could potentially be mistaken for pecans if you're not paying attention. One is the black walnut. They are both edible nuts, but the impostor has a very thick green husk that does not split when ripe.

Chia (Salvia columbariae)

Chia (*Salvia columbariae*).[48]

- **Distinct Characteristics:** Chia seeds are tiny, edible seeds from some species in the genus *Salvia*, which also includes sage (*S. officinalis*) and rosemary (*S. rosmarinus*). Golden chia (*S. columbarieae*) is native to the West, identified by its deeply dissected leaves and globular clusters of purple or pink flowers.

- **Preferred Habitats:** Chia plants are right at home in hot, arid climates. You'll find them in open, sunny areas like dry meadows, prairies, and even along roadsides.

- **Seasonal Nuances:** Chia plants are warm-weather annuals that sprout in the spring and mature by late summer.

- **Nutritional Benefits:** Chia seeds are revered as a superfood, and for good reason. They have it all – omega-3 fatty acids, protein, fiber, antioxidants, essential vitamins, and minerals – and in large quantities, too.

- **Identification Tips:** Look for the frilly, deeply dissected leaves and the spherical clusters of purple flowers, which make the plants looks like tiny Truffula trees!

- **Potential Lookalikes/Poisonous Counterparts:** Chia has a very distinctive appearance and no real lookalikes. Many species of sage (*Salvia* spp.) have similar flowers, but they are not arranged in round clusters like chia. Most sages smell minty or sage-like, but chia plants smell rather skunky – another distinctive feature.

Juniper Berries

Juniper berries.[49]

- **Distinct Characteristics:** Juniper berries are actually the small, blue-green to purple cones produced by different species of juniper (*Juniperus* spp.), especially common juniper (*J. communis*) and Rocky Mountain juniper (*J. scopulorum*). Junipers can be identified by their minute, scale-like needles, similar to cypresses (*Cupressus* spp.) but with smaller cones.

- **Preferred Habitats:** Juniper trees and shrubs are well-adapted to harsh, dryland conditions. You'll find them clinging to the slopes of canyons, lining the edges of high-altitude meadows, and even sprouting up in the cracks of outcroppings. They're not picky about where they grow as long as there's enough sun and well-draining soil.

- **Seasonal Nuances:** Junipers produce berries every year, but each berry takes over a year to ripen, so often both ripe and immature berries can be found on the same tree at different times of year. In most species, the berries ripen in autumn and winter, turning from green or blue to red or deep purple, and the best juniper berries are often harvested in the depths of winter.

- **Nutritional Benefits:** Juniper berries are far more than just a flavoring agent; they are rich in antioxidants, essential oils, vitamin C, vitamin A, and other B-complex vitamins.

- **Identification Tips:** A juniper tree can vary in size, from scraggly little bushes to 40-foot-tall giants. Unlike pines, firs, and other conifers, junipers have tiny scale-like leaves rather than needles. The berries are about a quarter inch in diameter and dark blue-black when ripe, though they usually appear light blue-green due to the waxy, resinous coating on the surface. When you cut them open, the berries should have one to three hard, nut-like seeds inside.

- **Potential Lookalikes/Poisonous Counterparts:** Junipers have no common lookalikes, but some ornamental junipers produce berries that are toxic even in moderate quantities, so only harvest berries from wild trees.

Black Walnuts

Black walnuts.[50]

- **Distinct Characteristics:** Black walnuts are large, dark-colored nuts produced by black walnut (*Juglans nigra*) trees, which are related to pecans and hickory (*Carya* spp.). The walnut fruits have a thick, green outer husk that will stain your fingers a dark brown when ripe. Inside the husk is the hard, brownish-black walnut shell that protects the nutmeat.

- **Preferred Habitats:** Black walnut trees grow in wet, well-draining soils along streams and rivers and in bottomland forests. They love areas with full sun exposure and prefer mildly acidic soils.

- **Seasonal Nuances:** Black walnuts form their green, golf ball-sized fruits in late summer. By early fall, the nuts will begin to fall, which is a great time to harvest them. The husks should still be green, but slightly squishy and soft enough to indent with your thumb. You can remove the husks before harvesting (you can use the heel of your boot, or even run them over with your car!) or leave them on, and wait to remove them until they turn brown.

- **Nutritional Benefits:** Black walnuts provide a good boost of protein, magnesium, phosphorus, copper, healthy fats, fiber, and B vitamins.

- **Identification Tips:** The leaves have 15, 17, or 19 leaflets, and give off a sharp (but not unpleasant) smell when crushed; some people describe it as similar to furniture polish.

- **Potential Lookalikes/Poisonous Counterparts:** While walnut trees can resemble pecan (*Carya illinoensis*) trees to the untrained eye, the nuts themselves are quite distinctive and have no real lookalikes. Arizona walnuts (*Juglans major*) are similar in appearance to black walnuts but much smaller, and the leaves usually have fewer than 15 leaflets.

Roots and Tubers

Burdock Root (*Arctium lappa*)

Burdock (*Arctium lappa*).[51]

- **Distinct Characteristics:** Burdock (*Arctium lappa*) is a large, biennial plant that can grow up to six feet tall, with enormous heart-shaped leaves that can reach over a foot long. The long, thick taproot is both edible and medicinal.

- **Preferred Habitats:** Burdock is a wild weed that is surprisingly widespread and very adaptable. It will grow happily in vacant lots, pastures, roadsides, and any sunny, open area with sufficient water.

- **Seasonal Nuances:** Burdock is a biennial, meaning it has a two-year lifecycle. In the first year, the plant's energy is aimed at establishing a strong root system and producing large, green leaves. During this first year, the root will grow long and thick with smooth skin. The best time to dig up and eat burdock root is in the fall of the first year after the leaves have died back but before the plant goes dormant for winter. In the second year, the energy in the roots is used to fuel flowering and seed production, and the roots from these plants will be less tender and flavorful.

- **Nutritional Benefits:** Burdock root is low in calories and high in fiber, vitamins A and C, iron, calcium, and potassium. It also contains inulin, a prebiotic fiber for healthy gut bacteria.

- **Identification Tips:** Burdock's large, heart-shaped leaves can grow to over two feet long and have an earthy, bitter scent that can only be described as "green". Burdock smells green. The roots should have a light brown or tan exterior without any major cuts, scrapes, or shriveled/damaged areas. Stay away from any roots that look old, discolored, or unhealthy.

- **Potential Lookalikes/Poisonous Counterparts:** Several species of dock (*Rumex* spp.) grow in similar habitats to burdock, and have large leaves that can resemble burdock's, especially bitter dock (*R. obtusifolius*). (In fact, its common name simply means "dock that produces burs".) Dock leaves are narrower overall, and never reach the enormous size of burdock leaves. They also have large taproots, but nowhere near as large as burdock roots.

Camas Lily Bulbs

Camas[52]

- **Distinct Characteristics:** The common camas (*Camassia quamash*) is a lily-like native perennial with edible bulbs that have been a staple for indigenous cultures throughout the continent. For most of the year the plants are relatively inconspicuous: not much more than a tuft of long, grass-like leaves. In late spring, however, they burst into bloom with showy purple flowers borne on stalks that can reach three feet tall. The bulbs, which resemble small potatoes, develop a few inches below the soil.

- **Preferred Habitats:** Camas lilies grow in open areas. In spring the plants need lots of water to bloom, but they are quite drought-tolerant outside of the flowering season. For this reason they can often be found in dry habitats that are seasonally wet, from prairies and hillsides to ephemeral pools and mountain streambanks.

- **Seasonal Nuances:** Camas bulbs are energy storage: think of them as solar "batteries" that the plants recharge each spring and summer. In early spring, these batteries are discharged to power the aboveground growth – which then recharges the battery as long as there's enough water for the plants to photosynthesize. This means that the bulbs will be sweetest and most nutritious between the end of one growing season and the beginning of the next. However, beginning foragers should only harvest from plants that still have spent flowers, as this is the only way to reliably distinguish them from their toxic lookalikes (see below).

- **Nutritional Benefits:** Camas bulbs are a good source of complex carbohydrates, fiber, calcium, iron, and potassium.

- **Identification Tips:** Camas plants have leaves up to two feet long but only about half an inch wide, and nearly always have 9 or fewer leaves per plant. The bulbs – technically modified stems called *corms* – are round and oblong, between half an inch and two inches in diameter. They are covered with papery brown skins, but should have firm white flesh. Don't take any bulbs that look shriveled, discolored, or have blemished flesh.

Death camas.[53]

- **Potential Lookalikes/Poisonous Counterparts:** The toxic death camas (*Toxicoscordion venenosum*) is the most common poisonous lookalike, but it is only one of a number of related species that can cause serious poisoning if ingested. Most of these have white or greenish-white flowers that can be distinguished easily from the blue/purple blooms of common camas. However, they are very difficult to distinguish without flowers, so beginning foragers should only harvest bulbs frrom plants with flowers.

Evening Primrose Roots

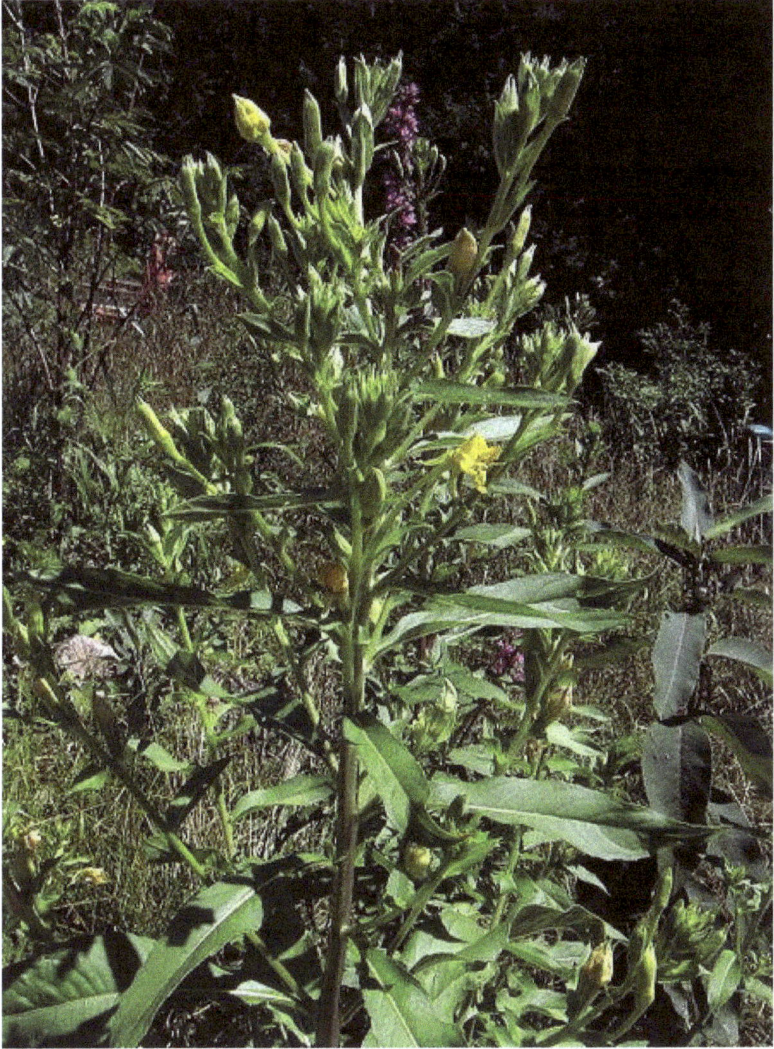

Evening primrose. [54]

- **Distinct Characteristics:** Evening primrose (Oenothera biennis) is a widespread biennial herb with edible carrot-like roots. First-year plants are inconspicuous rosettes of red-tinged leaves, but in the second year the plants bloom with bright yellow four-petaled flowers on stalks up to four feet high. Both the stem and the willow-like leaves are often tinged with red, and the flowers, true to the plant's name, open in the evening and close in the morning.

- **Preferred Habitats:** Evening primrose is a specialist of disturbed soils, both natural and man-made: forest clearings, pastures, roadsides and even vacant lots are all potential habitat for this plant, which is found in nearly every state in the lower 48.

- **Seasonal Nuances:** Evening primrose roots develop during the first year and overwinter, then fuel the plant's rapid growth in the second year. This means the roots of flowering plants won't be very good to eat, so only harvest roots from first-year plants. The best time to harvest is in the fall, after the growing season has ended but before the aboveground parts die back and make identification more challenging.

- **Nutritional Benefits:** Evening primrose roots are known for their high omega-6 fatty acids and antioxidant content.

- **Identification Tips:** Because second-year primroses are so much easier to spot than first-year plants, note any places you see them blooming abundantly and look nearby for rosettes. The flowers themselves are bright yellow and fairly large, but are most distinctive simply for their habit of remaining closed during the day. The lance-like leaves have a light-colored midrib and a reddish tinge at the base, and first-year plants will look like a bunch of these leaves stuck in the ground. The roots themselves are a couple of inches long and brown on the outside, but should have firm, bright white flesh.

- **Potential Lookalikes/Poisonous Counterparts:** A number of species of *Oenothera* resemble common evening primrose and also have edible roots. In the West, Hooker's evening primrose (*Oenothera elata*) is the most widespread; it tends to have much larger flowers (up to three inches in diameter), and while it often has a red stem like common evening primrose, its leaves are generally all green.

Wild Carrot Roots

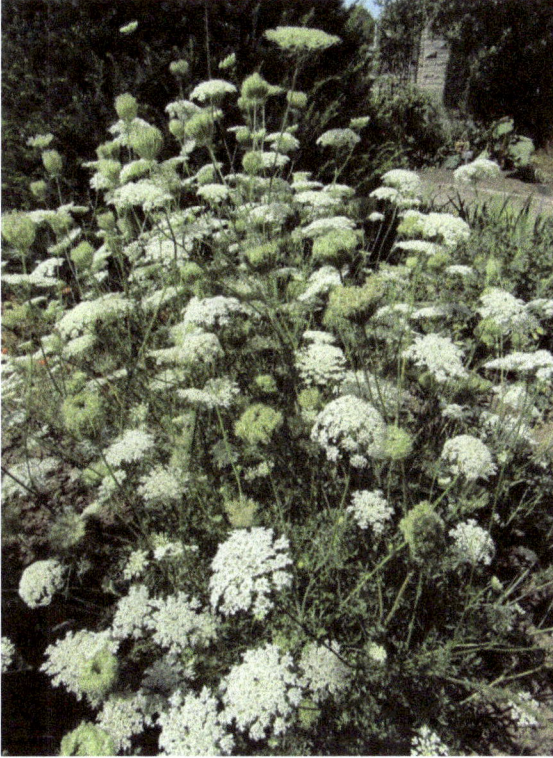

Wild carrot.[55]

- **Distinct Characteristics:** Also called Queen Anne's lace, wild carrots (*Daucus carota*) are easily identified by their large clusters of white flowers, each with a single purple flower in the center. The flowering stalks can reach three to four feet tall, and mature into fruit clusters that look like little birds' nests. Their long and tapered roots resemble those of their domesticated carrot cousins, though smaller and less colorful.

- **Preferred Habitats:** Wild carrots are an exotic species, native to Europe and western Asia. In North America they commonly colonize disturbed sites like pastures and vacant lots, as well as woodland edges.

- **Seasonal Nuances:** Like many plants with edible roots, wild carrots are biennials: in the first year, the plants remain rosettes of lacy, fern-like leaves, which persist throughout the growing season. The following summer, the plants bolt, producing tall, hollow stems topped with their distinctive umbrella-shaped flower heads. Like other biennial roots, they should be harvested in the fall of the first year.

- **Nutritional Benefits:** Just like regular carrots, wild carrots are sources of vitamin A, vitamin C, fiber, and potassium.

- **Identification Tips:** Wild carrot leaves are large, feathery, and smell like carrots, and the stems are usually hairy. The flower clusters nearly always have a single dark purple flower at the center, which is unique to the species.

- **Potential Lookalikes/Poisonous Counterparts:** Beginning foragers should exercise caution around wild carrot, as it closely resembles (and may be found growing alongside) poison hemlock (*Conium maculatum*). Poison hemlock is extremely toxic and can be fatal if consumed! Unlike wild carrot, poison hemlock leaves have a strongly unpleasant smell, and the stems are smooth -- never hairy -- and usually blotched with red or purple. Its flower clusters also lack a dark central flower, though it is not always present on wild carrots. Wild parsnip also looks like wild carrot, but is easier to distinguish: its leaves are much less "feathery" than wild carrot, and its flowers are yellow instead of white.

Dandelion Roots

Dandelion roots.[56]

- **Distinct Characteristics:** Dandelion roots are the long, tapered roots of the dandelion plant.
- **Preferred Habitats:** Dandelions will grow almost anywhere, but are especially common near human settlements: lawns, gardens, roadsides, pastures, and even sidewalks and parking lots.
- **Seasonal Nuances:** Dandelion roots can be harvested at any time of the year, but they are best collected after the plants have bloomed, when they are sending carbohydrates to the roots to prepare for winter.
- **Nutritional Benefits:** Dandelion roots are high in vitamins A, C, and K, as well as minerals such as iron, calcium, and potassium.
- **Identification Tips:** The roots are pale, with a reddish-brown exterior. They are fairly uniform in thickness throughout their length and exude a milky white liquid when you break or slice them.
- **Potential Lookalikes/Poisonous Counterparts:** Many plants in the sunflower family resemble dandelions, some quite closely: in the Mountain West, mountain dandelions (*Agoseris* spp.) are the most common and widespread. None are toxic, though they may be less palatable. Fortunately, dandelions can be reliably distinguished from all similar species by their hollow, unbranched flower stalks, which exude the same milky sap as the roots when broken.

Chapter 5: Mountain West Mushrooms

Without fungi, forests, as you know them, simply wouldn't exist. For some people, the thought of fungi probably conjures up images of slimy, smelly mushrooms sprouting in the damp corners of a garden after a heavy rain. You can't blame them; fungi don't have the most glamorous reputation. They're the underdogs, often overlooked and underappreciated, but their role in sustaining forest ecosystems is nothing short of essential. Without fungi, the whole system would grind to a halt. It would be like trying to bake a cake without any flour; it just wouldn't work.

Fungi are the great decomposers of the forest. Nobody goes to clean up the litter of dead leaves, branches, and even the trunks of fallen trees all over the forest floor, but somehow, they disappear. That's fungi that are hard at work, breaking down all that dead organic matter and recycling the nutrients back into the soil. It's a thankless job, but without it, the forests would be completely choked with decaying debris!

Fungi are the great decomposers of the forest.[57]

That's not all they do. Many species of fungi have formed intimate and mutually helpful relationships with the trees and other plants in the forest. In these symbiotic associations, also called mycorrhizal relationships, the fungi are the middlemen, connecting the plants to resources they can't easily access on their own. The plants, on the other hand, have sugar-rich sap that the fungi love to feed on. The fungi use their extensive underground networks to gather hard-to-reach nutrients and water and shuttle them back to the plants. In return, they get as much sap as they need.

Fungi have an incredible underground network of fungal threads, or hyphae, sprawling for acres and acres across the forest floor. Think secret internet for trees and plants – a "wood wide web," if you will. These fungal pathways connect the roots of different plants, allowing them to communicate with each other and share resources. It's wild to think about, but the trees send signals through this fungal network to warn each other of things like pests, drought, or other threats on the horizon. The fungi work as the information superhighway, ferrying nutrients and messages back and forth to keep the whole forest ecosystem in balance. Without these fungal connections, the forest would be a much lonelier, more fragile place!

Basic Mushroom Anatomy and Terminology

Mushrooms, a kind of fungi, are a lot more complex than those little buttons you see on your pizza. These fungi come in all shapes, sizes, and even colors. Some are big and pudgy, others are tiny and fragile, but they all have a few general body parts that tie them together.

The main visible part of a mushroom is the cap. A mushroom cap can be anything from smooth and arched to frilly and irregular. Underneath, you should find a stem holding the cap up, although there are mushrooms with no stem at all, where the cap is practically sitting right on the ground. Radiating out from the stem are the gills – paper-thin structures that produce the mushroom's spores. The color, spacing, and pattern of the gills are ways to identify different mushroom species. Spores are the mushroom's version of seeds. It is how it spreads and reproduces. Depending on the species, the spores might be white, brown, pink, or even purple. If you get up close, you might even see some thread-looking structures called hyphae, which make up the bulk of the mushroom's underground body.

Knowledge of basic mushroom anatomy is great, but what matters is being able to accurately identify different species. Not all mushrooms are the same, even if some look the same. Some are perfectly safe to eat, while others will make you seriously sick or even kill you. It's not worth the risk to go foraging for wild mushrooms unless you really know what you're doing. One wrong move, and you could end up in the hospital.

Tips for Mushroom Identification

- **Spore Color:** What is the color of the mushroom's spores? You'll know by conducting a spore test. Get a clean, light-colored piece of paper or a glass slide. Carefully remove the mushroom stem, leaving just the cap. Then place the cap, gill-side down, right in the middle of your paper or slide. Let it sit there for a few hours or overnight. During that time, the mushroom will slowly release its tiny spores, which will fall onto the test surface and make a print. Different species will leave behind spores of different colors, from pure white to deep purple-black. The color of the spore print can help you identify the mushroom species.

- **Cap Shape and Texture:** Check the shape and texture of the mushroom's cap. Is it flat, rounded, or umbrella-shaped? Is the surface smooth, scaly, or a bit slimy? Any unusual features, like warts or rings, are important clues about the type of mushroom you're handling.

- **Stem Characteristics:** Check the stem and look at the color, texture, and any weird bumps or rings. Some poisonous mushrooms have a bulbous base or a skirt on the stem. These details will help you distinguish between edible and non-edible varieties.

- **Gill Arrangement and Color:** The gills underneath the cap are also important. Poisonous mushrooms sometimes have gills that are unusually white, red, or suspiciously shiny. Also, look at how the gills are spaced and how they connect to the stem.

- **Habitat and Growth Patterns:** The location and surroundings where you find a mushroom might tell you what kind of mushroom it could be. Different mushrooms prefer specific types of habitats. Some like to grow near certain trees, while others love particular soil conditions. For instance, the mushroom you find under an oak tree is going to be a different type than the one you find growing in the grass. The way they are growing is another clue. Are they all by themselves, or are they clustered together in a big group? Some mushroom species are loners, while others grow in clusters.

- **Smell and Taste:** While you should never, ever taste or eat a mushroom that you are unsure of, the smell and taste are clues for identification. Some mushrooms have a particular smell, like the strong, unpleasant smell of the death cap or the fruity or anise-like scent of certain edible species.

- **Using Field Guides:** Always cross-reference your observations with reliable field guides or online resources that contain detailed descriptions and photos of different species of mushrooms. Don't rely on some random website or homemade guide that might steer you in the wrong direction. Get field guides that are written by actual experts, like mycologists or experienced mushroom foragers.

- **Join a Local Mycological Society:** As a member of a local mycological society, you get access to their collective wisdom. These people have spent years, if not decades, studying the mushrooms in that particular region. They know the ins and outs of which species grow where, what the key identifying features are, and which ones are safe to eat. Instead of staring at a mysterious mushroom and scratching your head, take your specimen to your local mycological society meeting, describe where you found it, and let the experts tell you what they know. Groups like these also organize foraging trips and workshops, where you can learn hands-on mushroom-hunting techniques from the experts. They'll show you the best places to search, how to properly harvest without damaging the fungal networks, and how to process and prepare whatever you find.

Safety Considerations

- **Proper Identification:** Accurately identifying mushroom species is an absolute must, with no exceptions. There are so many shapes, sizes, and colors it's easy to get them confused, especially if you're new to foraging. Don't put your money on a quick glance; cross-reference your findings against multiple field guides and speak with local mushroom experts for extra certainty.

- **Regional Variations:** What's considered safe and edible in one part of the world may be toxic in another. Mushroom species vary dramatically by geographic region, so don't assume a mushroom is safe to eat just because you've had it elsewhere. Always double-check local identification guides.

- **Toxic Lookalikes:** Even if you think you've identified an edible mushroom, make 100% sure it isn't a close lookalike that could be poisonous. Always double, triple, and quadruple-check those identifications.

- **Allergic Reactions:** A mushroom might be generally regarded as edible, but that doesn't mean your body is going to agree. Some people have had unexpected allergic reactions or personal sensitivities to certain fungal species, so when trying a new wild mushroom, always start small and pay attention to any unpleasant side effects before going all the way.

- **Cooking Considerations:** Some mushroom species become more poisonous when they're cooked, while others need extensive preparation to break down their toxins. It's not as simple as just sautéing them in a pan. You have to know the ins and outs of each mushroom's cooking requirements to make sure you're not putting yourself at risk.

Profiles of Common Edible Mushrooms

Morel Mushrooms (*Morchella* spp.)

Morel mushroom.[58]

- **Description:** Morel mushrooms (genus *Morchella*) are some of the most recognizable mushrooms in the wild. They have a spongy, honeycomb-shaped cap that is two to five inches tall and one to three inches wide. It is attached to a white or pale, hollow stem. The cap itself can be anything from pale yellow to dark brown, depending on the specific morel species.

- **Habitat:** You should find morels growing near the base of elm, ash, oak, and aspen trees in areas that have been recently disturbed by fire, logging, or other kinds of land management activities.

- **Seasonal Nuances:** The timing of the morel season is closely tied to spring rains and soil temperatures, so the exact timing could fluctuate from year to year.

- **Nutritional Benefits:** Morels are low in calories and a good source of protein, fiber, vitamin D, potassium, and selenium.

- **Identification Tips:** Morels look a little like strange toadstools, with a white stem and a cap covered in honeycomb-like chambers. Look a little closer, though, and you won't see any gills, because the cap is fused to the stem; stranger still, the whole mushroom is hollow! If you can remember that morels always have fused caps and hollow stems, it will be a lot harder to be fooled by lookalikes.

False morel.[59]

- **Potential Lookalikes/Poisonous Counterparts:** The only mushrooms that remotely resemble morels are so-called "false morels" (*Gyromitra* and *Verpa* spp.), some of which are closely related. Their stems may have empty spaces inside, but are never completely hollow, and their caps – which are wrinkly, but not chambered – aren't fused to the stem, but only attached at the top.

Oyster Mushrooms

Oyster mushroom (*Pleurotus ostreatus*).[60]

- **Distinct Characteristics:** Oyster mushrooms (*Pleurotus ostreatus*) have a fan-shaped or oyster-looking cap that is white, gray, yellow, blue, or pale beige. The caps are soft, velvety, fragile, and slightly sweet. The stems are short and tend to be an extension of the cap rather than a separate structure.

- **Habitat:** These mushrooms grow in clusters on dead or decaying trunks of hardwood trees such as oak, maple, and beech.

- **Seasonal Nuances:** Late summer is when you'll see the first flush of oyster mushrooms, especially after some good soaking rains. You can harvest them then all the way into mid-fall. You may still find some toward the end of fall, but the harvest will become more sporadic.

- **Nutritional Benefits:** Oyster mushrooms are low in calories but high in protein and fiber.

- **Identification Tips:** Oyster mushrooms grow in large clusters that emerge from a single point on a tree or fallen log. The caps are asymmetrical, often shaped like a kidney or oyster shell, and often have a silvery or shiny appearance. The gills on the underside extend partway down the stem, and turn yellow as the spores develop. The whole mushroom has a mild, slightly sweet smell that is distinctive once you get to know it.

Jack-o'-lantern mushroom (*Omphalotus olearius*).[61]

- **Potential Lookalikes/Poisonous Counterparts:** There aren't many gilled mushrooms that look like oysters, and even fewer that grow directly on trees. Jack-o-lantern mushrooms (*Omphalotus* spp.), which are mildly toxic, can be mistaken for oysters because they grow in clusters from dead wood, and also have gills that extend down the stem. However, they are bright orange all over, while the stems and flesh of oyster mushrooms are white. If you see oyster musrooms

Porcini (*Boletus edulis*)

Porcini.[62]

- **Distinct Characteristics:** Porcini mushrooms (*Boletus edulis*), also called ceps and king boletes, are the most sought-after type of bolete mushroom. They are known for their large, fleshy caps that span the color spectrum from white to dark brown. These caps feel like suede and grow as large as 12 inches in diameter.

- **Habitat:** In damp forests, porcini mushrooms should be found attached to the roots of coniferous and deciduous trees, such as pine, fir, spruce, and oak.

- **Seasonal Nuances:** The porcini mushroom season in the Mountain West generally runs from mid-summer to early fall, with the peak occurring in August and September.

- **Nutritional Benefits:** Porcini mushrooms provide a good amount of protein, fiber, and vitamin D.

- **Identification Tips:** In North America, porcini mushrooms almost always grow under pines and other conifers. Their caps can be tan to brown and look a little like dinner rolls - seriously! The caps are often slightly sticky, especially in humid weather – though if the cap is slimy, it means the mushroom is starting to decay. The stems are very thick compared to other boletes, especially when young, and have a net-like pattern of ridges on the top half. The flesh should be pure white all the way through, and will not change color after being touched.

Rubroboletus eastwoodiae, a common and mildly toxic bolete. Note the blue-stained flesh, which changes color when bruised or cut.[68]

- **Potential Lookalikes/Poisonous Counterparts:** There are many species of bolete, and many of them are either unpalatable or toxic, so take care with your identification. Most can be easily distinguished, as they are differently colored: red caps instead of tan, yellow stems instead of white, and so on. Many also have flesh or spores that turn blue when exposed to air – it should go without saying, but don't eat these! The one most likely to cause trouble is the false king bolete, which superficially resembles porcinis in size and color. Their stems have no net-like pattern, or at most a little below the stem, and their flesh actually DOES turn blue when bruised, but impatient foragers may not notice, as it can take a half hour or longer and may be rather faint.

Matsutake (*Tricholoma matsutake*)

Matsutake (*Tricholoma matsutake*).[64]

- **Distinct Characteristics:** Matsutake mushrooms (*Tricholoma matsutake*) have a robust, fleshy cap that could be reddish-brown to pale tan. The cap is dome-shaped when the mushroom is young, gradually flattening out as the mushroom matures.

- **Habitat:** Matsutakes grow in areas with mature coniferous forests, particularly pine, fir, or cedar trees. It grows solitary or in small clusters, nestled among the leaf litter and pine needles on the forest floor.

- **Seasonal Nuances:** Matsutake mushrooms make their appearance in late summer and early fall, with the peak season running from August through October.
- **Nutritional Benefits:** Matsutakes are a rich source of protein, dietary fiber, vitamin D, riboflavin, and niacin.
- **Identification Tips:** The matsutake stem is very thick and fibrous. It should be partially embedded right into the soil, giving the base a bit of a bulbous look. The stem color is generally a clean whitish tone, although it may pick up some brown or reddish tones as the mushroom gets older. Also, feel the stem to see if you pick up on a scaly texture along its length. The most distinctive trait of the matsutake is its smell, which is pungent and spicy - many people compare it to cinnamon. This strong, spicy scent is unique among mushrooms, and you should only harvest specimens you can tell by smell!

Death cap (*Amanita phalloides*).[65]

- **Potential Lookalikes/Poisonous Counterparts:** Watch out for the death cap (*Amanita phalloides*). This mushroom might look a like the matsutake because they both have brownish cap colors and thick, fibrous stems. However, the death cap is lighter in color overall, with a more slender stem and a volva – a sac at the base of the stem, that looks like an egg the mushroom hatched from, Matsutake has a thick, rooting stem but no volva. The death cap also smells very different: young specimens smell sweet, but as they age this changes to a sickening smell that should warn you off eating it.

Crown coral Mushroom (*Artomyces pyxidatus*)

Coral fungi.[66]

- **Distinct Characteristics:** Crown coral mushrooms are best described as alien. Their branches resemble a bundle of slim tentacles reaching up from the forest floor, each with topped with a crown-like ring of even smaller branches that gives the fungus its name.
- **Habitat:** Crown coral mushrooms are among the few coral mushrooms that grow directly on the dead wood of deciduous trees: aspens, poplars, willows, and maples are among the most common hosts.

- **Seasonal Nuances:** The best time to harvest crown coral mushrooms is from late summer to early fall.

- **Nutritional Benefits:** Crown coral mushrooms are low in calories but high in vitamin C, potassium, and selenium.

- **Identification Tips:** Crown coral mushrooms appear very different from most other mushrooms: true to their name, they look more like a coral than a fungus, with profusely branching stems that are topped with "crowns" of three to six tiny branches. Crown coral mushrooms are also tough and slightly brittle, not spongy.

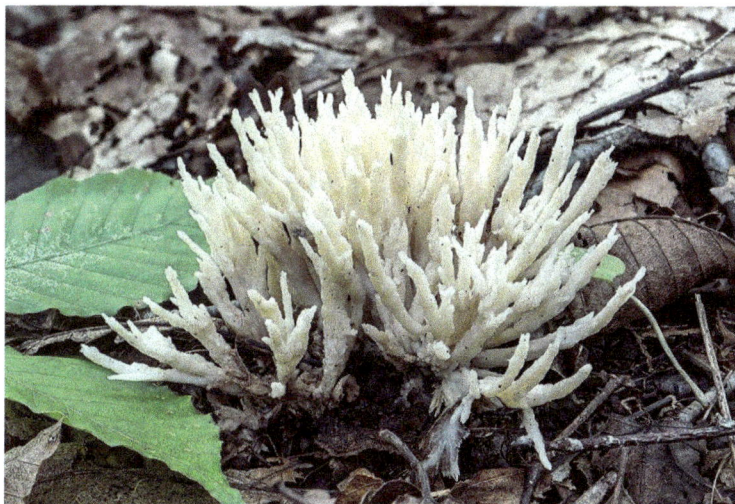

False coral fungus. [67]

- **Potential Lookalikes/Poisonous Counterparts:** There are many species of coral mushrooms that look like the crown coral mushroom: some are edible, some not. Most grow from leaf litter or organic matter in the soil, so sticking with specimens growing on logs will help you avoid many potential lookalikes. Other "false corals" can be identified by their odd colors, or because their branches have no crowns. Fortunately, only a few species are truly toxic, and none are found in the Mountain West.

Lobster Mushrooms

Lobster mushroom (*Hypomyces lactifluorum*).[68]

- **Distinct Characteristics:** The lobster mushroom (*Hypomyces lactifluorum*) isn't actually a mushroom; it is a parasitic fungus that has hijacked and transformed another mushroom species, either a *Russula* or *Lactarius* species. The parasite infects these mushrooms, softens them, and gives them a red-and-white coloring reminiscent of cooked lobster, as well as a flavor that has been described as strikingly similar.

- **Habitat:** Lobster mushrooms prefer old-growth coniferous and mixed forests that have spruce, fir, or pine trees.

- **Seasonal Nuances:** The parasite infects the mushrooms in early spring and summer. By mid-to-late summer, the infection slowly spreads until the hosts are completely red. Lobster mushrooms should be ready for harvest in early summer to early winter.

- **Nutritional Benefits:** Lobster mushrooms contain copper, some fiber, and tiny amounts of vitamins B and D.

- **Identification Tips:** Many different species of mushrooms can be parasitized by the lobster mushroom fungus, so they vary quite a bit in size and shape. The main thing to look for is the bright red-orange color, which is caused by the parasitic fungus. It covers the stem, gills, and caps, leaving the whole musroom a uniform color. Just like real lobsters, though, the mushrooms aren't red all the way through: cut one in half and you'll see it's just a thin coating over a mushroom that is white all the way through.

- **Potential Lookalikes/Poisonous Counterparts:** Lobster mushrooms have no true lookalikes: other mushrooms may have red caps, like the fly agaric (*Amanita muscaria*), or red stems, like the Satan's bolete (*Rubroboletus satanas*), but they won't be bright red all over – and if you cut them open, you'll see that the coloring extends at least part of the way into the flesh as well.

Cauliflower Mushrooms

Cauliflower mushroom (*Sparassis crispa*)[69]

- **Distinct Characteristics:** Cauliflower mushrooms (*Sparassis crispa*) grow four to 10 inches wide and have a neatly clustered, convoluted cap that matches the florets of their namesake vegetable. The caps are white to pale gray in color, sometimes showing hints of yellow or brown as they age.

- **Habitat:** Cauliflower mushrooms will be found in clusters at the bases or stumps of hardwood trees, especially oaks, aspens, and maples.

- **Seasonal Nuances:** Cauliflower mushrooms are visible on the forest floor in late summer, around August or September, when the temperatures cool and the rains pick up, but just as quickly as they arrive, they vanish. Your best bet for finding them is after heavy rainfall.

- **Nutritional Benefits:** Cauliflower mushrooms contain high amounts of vitamin D and fair levels of B vitamins, copper, and selenium.

- **Identification Tips:** The most defining characteristic is the complex, brain-looking structure of the cap. Unlike many other mushrooms that have a smooth, rounded top, the cauliflower's cap is a cluster of wavy, frilly lobes. The stem is very short and thick – more like a stalk than a traditional mushroom stem. Older cauliflower mushrooms should look cream or beige, but never gray or other darker tones that you might see in some other wild mushroom species.

- **Potential Lookalikes/Poisonous Counterparts:** This is a beginner mushroom with no true lookalikes or toxic twins. When you see it, you'll know. *The only problem is actually seeing it!*

Shaggy Mane (*Coprinus comatus*)

- **Distinct Characteristics:** The shaggy mane gets its name from the shaggy, bell-shaped cap that comes up from the ground. The cap starts off white but quickly turns inky black and softens as it matures, almost as if it's melting. The stem is long and slim, growing up to six inches tall, with a ring-like skirt around the middle. As the cap opens up, you'll notice dark gills that start white but quickly turn black.

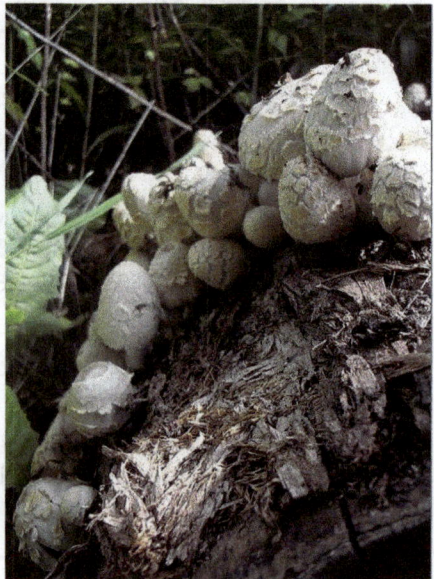

Shaggy mane (*Coprinus comatus*).[70]

- **Habitat:** Shaggy manes love grassy, disturbed areas like lawns, gardens, and along roadsides. They prefer humid weather and are likely to show up shortly after a good rain.

- **Seasonal Nuances:** Shaggy manes are visible in the fall after the first heavy rains of the season. They have a relatively short window of maturity because the caps turn to black, inky liquid as they age. The best time to harvest them is when the caps are still young and egg-shaped before self-destructing.

- **Nutritional Benefits:** Shaggy mane mushrooms are a reliable source of fiber and proteins.

- **Identification Tips:** The cap of the shaggy mane looks like an unopened umbrella: long and narrow, closely fitted to the stem (which is hollow), and distinctively scaly or shaggy. Newly emerged mushrooms actually look more like Q-tips than umbrellas, and by the time the cap starts to open, it will already be turning inky black and gooey at the edges. The whole mushroom will emerge, open, and melt into an unrecognizable puddle of inky slime in the space of an afternoon. Though older specimens don't look very appetizing, you can still eat them, and some foragers even say they taste better!

Destroying angel (*Amanita virosa*).[71]

- **Potential Lookalikes/Poisonous Counterparts:** The most problematic lookalike is the destroying angel (*Amanita virosa*). This mushroom is completely white, just like the shaggy mane, so you can mistake one for the other, but the destroying angel's cap is smooth and much more open; if you look beneath it you'll see a thin "skirt" of tissue just below the cap, which shaggy manes do not have.

Chicken-of-the-Woods

Chicken of the woods (*Laetiporus sulphureus*).[73]

- **Distinct Characteristics:** Also known as the sulfur shelf or the tree chicken, this mushroom is hard to mistake for anything else when you know what you're looking for. The name "chicken-of-the-woods" comes from the mushroom's uncanny resemblance to cooked chicken, both in texture and flavor.

- **Habitat:** Chicken-of-the-woods grows primarily on hardwoods, especially oak (*Quercus*), beech (*Fagus*), and poplar (*Populus*). It occasionally grows on conifers as well, especially hemlock (*Tsuga*), but mushrooms growing on these trees may be toxic and should be avoided.

- **Seasonal Nuances:** Chicken-of-the-woods fruits from late spring to fall, emerging from the same spot on the tree year after year (generally at head height or higher). They are best early in the season, when the caps are young, firm, and vividly colored; as they mature, they harden and become less palatable.

- **Nutritional Benefits:** Chicken-of-the-woods is one of the best protein sources, containing 20 to 30% protein by dry weight. They also contain antioxidants and prebiotic fiber.

- **Identification Tips:** Its incredible color is probably the first thing you'll notice. Chicken-of-the-woods have nearly fluorescent orange-yellow caps that look unnatural. The caps themselves grow quite large, sometimes reaching over a foot in width when fully mature. You'll find them in overlapping, tiered clusters or "shelves" that protrude from the sides of tree trunks, stumps, or fallen logs. The underside has tiny, barely visible pores rather than gills, which helps differentiate it from some lookalike species. You'll almost always find chicken-of-the-woods growing right on the trunks or stumps of hardwood trees, never on the ground, and the specific tree host will also help confirm the identification.

- **Potential Lookalikes/Poisonous Counterparts:** Chicken of the woods is almost impossible to mistake for anything else. A few species of shelf fungi might have bands of colors that appear superficially similar, like the turkey tail (*Trametes versicolor*), but none have the distinctive combination of bright orange caps with yellow edges. None are toxic, though few of them are considered edible due to their tough, woody flesh.

Toxic Mushrooms of the Mountain West

- ### Death Cap
  The death cap is one of the deadliest mushrooms in the world. It grows near the roots of oak, pine, and other hardwood trees, just waiting to trick unsuspecting foragers. Its cap is smooth, pale green to white, and can grow as big as 12 inches wide. The stem is also white and tall, with an obvious ring around it. Underneath the cap, you'll find white gills that are free from the stem. The biggest clue that you're looking at a death cap is the large, skirt-

like ring or "death cap" at the base of the stem. This ring is a remnant of the universal veil that enclosed the immature mushroom.

- **Destroying Angel**

True to its name, the destroying angel is completely white in color, from the smooth, rounded cap to the thick, tall stem. There is no big, obvious ring here, but it has a thin, fragile skirt higher up on the stem. Importantly, the gills are also white and free from the stem. This all-white outfit makes it easy to confuse with edible mushrooms like the meadow mushroom or shaggy manes. Keep an eye out for this trickster in coniferous or mixed forests.

- **Galerina Marginata**

Also known as the funeral bell, this little brown mushroom is extremely poisonous. The funeral bell has a small, brown, convex cap that becomes flatter as it matures. The gills are rust-brown, and the stem is also thin and brown – usually with a little skirt. This nondescript little mushroom is nearly identical to the edible honey fungus, save for the brown spore print it leaves behind (honey fungus has white spore prints). Galerina species grow in clusters at the base of trees or on decaying wood.

Deadly galerina (*Galerina marginata*).[73]

Tips for Sustainable Harvesting

- When you harvest, gently twist and pull the mushroom caps. Leave the underground fungus network (mycelium) intact so the mushrooms can keep growing.

- Only take a small portion of the mushrooms you find. Leave plenty behind so there's enough for everyone, including the wildlife.

- Harvest in the morning or evening when the mushrooms are fresh. Avoid picking during the hot midday sun when they might be drying out.

- Learn when your preferred mushrooms emerge so you only collect them when they're in their prime.

- Cutting the mushroom stems with a knife is better than pulling them up. This keeps the underground network intact.

- When you're out foraging, step only on paths or rocks. Don't trample all over the forest floor and compact the soil, as that could hurt the fungi.

- When you're collecting, fan out and cover more ground instead of staying in one place. That way, you don't strip an entire area bare.

- Brush off any dirt, but wait to wash the mushrooms until you're ready to cook them. Washing too soon makes them go bad faster.

- If you find a mushroom you can't identify, take some photos and let the local mushroom experts know. They might be able to tell you more.

- If you want to, report your mushroom sightings and foraging data to online citizen science projects. That information helps researchers study fungal ecosystems.

Chapter 6: Cooking Wild Edibles: 12 Easy Recipes

You just returned home with a basket full of greens, mushrooms, roots, and berries, so what's next? Cooking and eating, obviously. Once your edible plants are positively ID'd, the actual cooking part is pretty straightforward. Wild greens, flowers, and berries are naturally more delicate than their cultivated counterparts, so they just need minimal cooking to bring out their flavors. Roots and mushrooms may require a little more prep work, but the meal itself is worth the effort.

Create the most delicious meals by using your freshly foraged goods.[74]

Here are a few general tips for cooking with wild plants:

- Give your foraged finds a good wash to remove dirt, bugs, or other unwanted bits. A salad spinner is great for greens.
- Use your wild ingredients quickly. They are more perishable than store-bought produce, so eat them or preserve them ASAP.
- Start slow when trying a new wild food. Some plants can cause digestive issues, especially if you're not adapted to them.
- Experiment with different cooking techniques like sautéing, steaming, or pickling.
- When in doubt, do NOT eat it.

12 Easy Recipes

Dandelion Flower Pancakes

Dandelion flower pancakes.[75]

Ingredients:

- 1 cup of all-purpose flour
- 2 tsp. of baking powder
- 1 tbsp. of sugar
- 1/2 tsp. of salt
- 1 cup of milk
- 1 egg
- 2 tbsp. of melted butter
- 1 cup of dandelion flowers

Instructions:

1. Whisk the flour, baking powder, sugar, and salt in a bowl.
2. In a separate bowl, beat the milk, egg, and melted butter.
3. Pour the wet ingredients into the dry ones and stir just until combined (don't overmix).
4. Fold in the dandelion flower petals.
5. Heat a lightly oiled pan over medium heat.
6. Scoop the batter by quarter cupfuls onto the hot surface. Cook for 2 to 3 minutes per side until they're golden brown.
7. Serve warm with your favorite pancake toppings.

Chokeberry Chutney

Ingredients:

- 2 cups of chokeberries, washed and stems removed
- 1 cup of apple cider vinegar
- ½ cup of brown sugar
- 1 diced small onion
- 2 minced cloves of garlic
- 1 tsp. of ground ginger
- ½ tsp. of ground cinnamon
- ¼ tsp. of ground cloves
- ¼ tsp. of salt

Instructions:

1. Pour all the ingredients into a medium saucepan and mix.

2. Bring to a boil over medium-high heat, then reduce to low heat.

3. Simmer for 20 to 25 minutes, stirring occasionally until the berries have broken down and the chutney has thickened.

4. Let it cool completely before transferring to a sealed container.

5. It will keep in the refrigerator for up to two weeks.

Root Vegetable Stew

Ingredients:

- 2 tbsp. of olive oil
- 1 diced onion
- 3 cloves of garlic, minced
- 1 lb. of assorted wild roots (burdock, wild carrot, sunchokes, etc.), peeled and chopped
- 4 cups of vegetable or bone broth
- 1 bay leaf
- 1 tsp. of dried thyme
- 1 tsp. of salt
- ½ tsp. of black pepper

Instructions:

1. Heat the olive oil in a large pot or Dutch oven over medium heat.

2. Add the onion and garlic and cook for 2 to 3 minutes until you get that sweet onion scent.

3. Stir in the chopped wild roots, broth, bay leaf, thyme, salt, and pepper.

4. Leave it to boil, then reduce the heat and simmer for 25 to 30 minutes until the roots are very soft.

5. Remove the bay leaf. Taste and adjust the seasoning as needed.

6. Serve hot, garnished with fresh herbs if you like.

Wild Onion Fritters

Ingredients:

- 1 cup of wild onions, ramps, or chives, finely chopped
- 1 cup of all-purpose flour
- 1 tsp. of baking powder
- ½ tsp. of salt
- ¼ tsp. of black pepper
- 1 egg
- ½ cup of milk
- Vegetable oil for frying
- Yogurt-herb dipping sauce:
- 1 cup of plain yogurt
- 2 tbsp. of chopped fresh herbs (dill, parsley, chives)
- 1 tbsp. of lemon juice
- ¼ tsp. of salt

Instructions:

1. Make the dipping sauce by mixing all the ingredients in a small bowl. Cover and chill until you are ready to use.
2. Whisk the flour, baking powder, salt, and pepper in a bowl.
3. Get a separate bowl and beat the egg and milk together.
4. Mix the wet and dry ingredients thoroughly. Fold in the chopped wild onions.
5. In a large pan, heat the vegetable oil over medium-high heat.
6. Scoop the batter by heaping tablespoonfuls and carefully place it in the hot oil. Fry for 2 to 3 minutes per side until it looks golden brown.
7. Drain the fritters on a paper towel-lined plate and serve warm with the yogurt dipping sauce.

Forest Berry Crisps

Ingredients:

- 2 cups of wild berries, washed and stemmed
- ½ cup of all-purpose flour
- ½ cup of old-fashioned oats
- ⅓ cup of brown sugar
- ¼ cup of cold, cubed, unsalted butter
- ¼ tsp. of ground cinnamon
- ¼ tsp. of salt

Instructions:

1. Preheat the oven to 375°F. Grease an 8x8-inch baking dish.
2. Chop the wild berries into a bowl.
3. Get another bowl and mix the flour, oats, brown sugar, cinnamon, and salt. Cut in the cold butter using a fork, pastry cutter, or clean hands until the mixture looks like coarse crumbs.
4. Spread the berries in the prepared baking dish. Top it evenly with the crumb topping.
5. Bake for 30 to 35 minutes or until the topping is golden brown and the juices are bubbling.
6. Let it cool for 15 minutes before serving.

Morel Mushroom Soup

Morel mushroom soup.[76]

Ingredients:

- 2 tbsp. of unsalted butter
- 1 diced onion
- 3 minced cloves of garlic
- 1 lb. of fresh morel mushrooms, halved or quartered if large
- 4 cups of chicken or vegetable broth
- 1 cup of half-and-half
- 2 tsp. of dried thyme
- 1 tsp. of salt
- ½ tsp. of black pepper

Instructions:

1. Melt the butter in a large pot over medium heat. Add the onion and garlic and cook for 3 to 4 minutes.
2. Stir in the morel mushrooms and cook for 5 to 7 minutes.
3. Pour in the broth and wait until it simmers. Reduce heat and let the soup cook for 15 minutes.
4. Stir in the half-and-half, thyme, salt, and pepper. Taste and adjust the spice to suit your palate.
5. Serve hot, garnished with extra thyme, chives, or anything you like.

Wild Strawberry Sorbet

Ingredients:

- 2 cups of wild strawberries, washed and hulled
- ¾ cup of granulated sugar
- 2 tbsp. of fresh lemon juice

Instructions:

1. Puree the strawberries in a food processor or blender until you get a smooth paste.
2. Mix the strawberry puree, sugar, and lemon juice in a saucepan and place over medium heat, stirring occasionally until the sugar has completely dissolved.

3. Pour the mixture into a shallow baking dish and freeze for 2 hours, stirring every 30 minutes until it shows signs of setting at the edges.

4. Transfer the partially frozen sorbet to a food processor and blend it until it is smooth and creamy.

5. Return the sorbet to the baking dish and continue freezing for another 2 to 3 hours until it is completely frozen.

6. Serve immediately, or store in an airtight container in the freezer for up to 2 weeks.

Juniper Berry Gin Fizz

Ingredients:

- ½ cup of fresh juniper berries, crushed
- 1 cup of gin
- ¼ cup of honey
- 1 cup of club soda
- Lemon wedges for serving

Instructions:

1. Pour the crushed juniper berries into a jar or airtight container. Add the gin. Seal and let it infuse for 24 to 48 hours in the refrigerator.

2. Strain the gin through a fine mesh sieve, pressing on the berries to extract as much liquid as possible. Throw away the solids.

3. Stir the infused gin and honey in a pitcher until the honey has fully dissolved.

4. Fill glasses with ice and pour the gin mixture over the top. Top each glass with club soda and a lemon wedge.

Garlic Butter Oyster Mushrooms

Ingredients:

- 1 lb. of fresh oyster mushrooms, cleaned and torn or sliced into bite-sized pieces
- 3 tbsp. of unsalted butter
- 3 minced cloves of garlic

- 1 tsp. of dried thyme
- ¼ tsp. of red pepper flakes (optional)
- Salt and black pepper for seasoning
- Chopped fresh parsley for garnish

Instructions:

1. Melt the butter in a pan over medium-high heat. Add the minced garlic and sauté for 1 minute until you can smell it.
2. Add the torn or sliced oyster mushrooms to the pan. Sauté for 5 to 7 minutes, turning at intervals until the mushrooms are soft and starting to brown.
3. Sprinkle in the dried thyme and red pepper flakes (if using). Season generously with salt and black pepper.
4. Continue cooking for another 2 to 3 minutes, giving the mushrooms time to soak up the garlic-herb butter sauce.
5. Remove it from the heat and transfer the buttered oyster mushrooms to a serving dish.
6. Garnish with chopped fresh parsley, and serve immediately with crusty bread, roasted meats, or your favorite sides.

Chia Seed Pudding

Chia seed pudding.[77]

Ingredients:

- ¼ cup of chia seeds
- 1½ cups of milk (dairy, plant-based, etc.)

- 2-3 tbsp. of maple syrup or honey
- 1 tsp. of vanilla extract
- ¼ tsp. of ground cinnamon (optional)
- Fresh fruit, nuts, coconut, or other toppings (optional)

Instructions:

1. Pour the chia seeds, milk, maple syrup/honey, and vanilla extract into a bowl and mix well.
2. Stir in the ground cinnamon if you're using it.
3. Cover the bowl and refrigerate for at least 4 hours or overnight. The chia seeds will thicken the mixture to a pudding consistency.
4. Once it's thickened, give the pudding a final stir. Taste and add more sweetener if you like.
5. Scoop the chia pudding into separate serving bowls or cups.
6. Top with your choice of fresh fruit, nuts, coconut, or any other toppings.
7. Serve chilled. Leftovers will be kept in the fridge for up to 5 days.

Pickled Wild Onions

Ingredients:

- 1 lb. of fresh wild onions, trimmed and sliced into ¼-inch rounds
- 1 cup of apple cider vinegar
- ¼ cup of water
- 2 tbsp. of granulated sugar
- 2 tsp. of kosher salt
- 1 tsp. of whole black peppercorns
- 2 bay leaves

Instructions:

1. Put the sliced wild onions into a bowl.
2. Add the vinegar, water, sugar, and salt to a saucepan and leave to boil. Stir as it boils to dissolve the sugar.
3. Remove the vinegar mixture from the heat and pour it over the wild onions. Add the peppercorns and bay leaves.

4. Let the onions cool completely at room temperature, then cover and refrigerate for at least 2 hours or up to 1 week.

5. The pickled onions will be stored in the refrigerator for up to one month.

Sautéed Chicken of the Woods

Ingredients:

- 1 lb. of chicken-of-the-woods mushrooms, cleaned and sliced
- 2 tbsp. of butter
- 2 minced cloves of garlic
- 1 tsp. of fresh thyme leaves
- Salt and pepper for seasoning
- Chopped parsley for garnish (optional)

Instructions:

1. Melt your butter in a pan over medium-high heat.

2. Add the sliced chicken-of-the-woods and sauté for 5 to 7 minutes or until they look brown.

3. Stir in the minced garlic and thyme. Cook for 2 more minutes.

4. Season with as much salt and pepper as you want.

5. Take it off the heat and transfer it to a serving dish.

6. Garnish with chopped parsley if you want, and serve as a side dish or an addition to other recipes.

Chapter 7: Medicinal Plants of the Mountain West

The use of plants for healing has its roots deeply embedded in the history of many ancient cultures all over the world. Human ancestors have been turning to the natural world for healing remedies for longer than you can possibly imagine. They appreciated the intrinsic properties and powers of herbs and flowers long before modern medicine came along. Look at the Ebers Papyrus, for example. It's an ancient Egyptian medical text that dates back to 1550 BCE, and it has over 800 different plant-based remedies documented in it. There is also Traditional Chinese Medicine (TCM), a practice fiercely dedicated to using herbal concoctions to bring the body back into balance that has been around for centuries. Ancient cultures understood how the energetic and therapeutic properties of different plants could help people feel their best. They didn't have modern medicine back then, but they had an extraordinary wealth of plant-based wisdom from which they were not afraid to draw. A lot of that knowledge has been passed down and is still relevant today, even as the healthcare system is now very tech-driven and pharmaceutical-focused.

Herbal and plant-based remedies are designed to help your body heal itself.[78]

As an alternative to just popping a pill to mask the symptoms, herbal and plant-based remedies are designed to help your body heal itself. Unbelievable, isn't it? These therapies recognize that the body, mind, and spirit are all connected, so they work to address the root causes of the problem, not just put a Band-Aid on it. Thankfully, a lot of this ancient plant wisdom is now being backed up by modern scientific research, so maybe people can learn a thing or two from our plant-loving ancestors and reconsider the potency of nature's pharmacy.

Now, if you're thinking, "Aren't plants just as risky as pharmaceuticals?" You're not wrong. Just like any drug, medicinal plants can definitely pose some risks if they're not used responsibly. Many of these herbs and botanicals have been safely used for ages, but even the ancients knew to make sure they understood what they were dealing with before trying anything new. That's why it's necessary to work closely with a qualified healthcare provider, like a licensed herbalist or naturopathic doctor, before adding any plant-based remedies to your routine. Self-diagnosis and self-medication are dangerous, especially where powerful natural medicines are concerned. You could end up with painful side effects or unfortunate interactions if you don't know what you're doing. So please, do your research, get professional help, and always put your safety first.

Medicinal Plants of the Mountain West

Yarrow

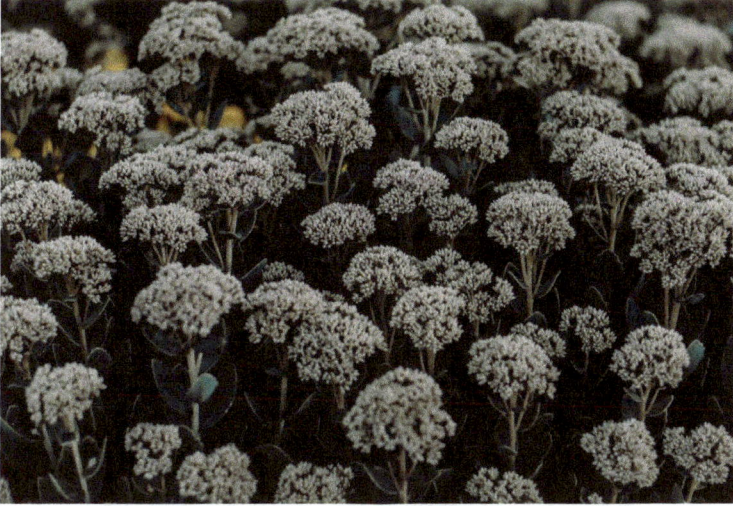

Yarrow.[79]

- **Description:** Yarrow is one of the common wildflowers you see all over the hills and meadows of the Mountain West. It can grow up to three feet tall, with finely divided, feathery-green leaves that give the plant a lacy, ferny appearance. The leaves smell like earth and spice, and in the summer, the plant produces small, white (or sometimes pink, purple, or yellow) flower heads at the top of the stem. These flower heads are flat and umbrella-shaped.

- **Therapeutic Properties:** Yarrow contains flavonoids and salicylates that give it anti-inflammatory, astringent, and antiseptic properties.

- **Traditional Uses:** Yarrow is great for stopping bleeding and digestive issues like stomachaches or diarrhea, relieving menstrual cramps, and bringing down fevers or general inflammation. The astringent qualities also make it good for treating minor cuts, scrapes, and skin irritations.

Arnica

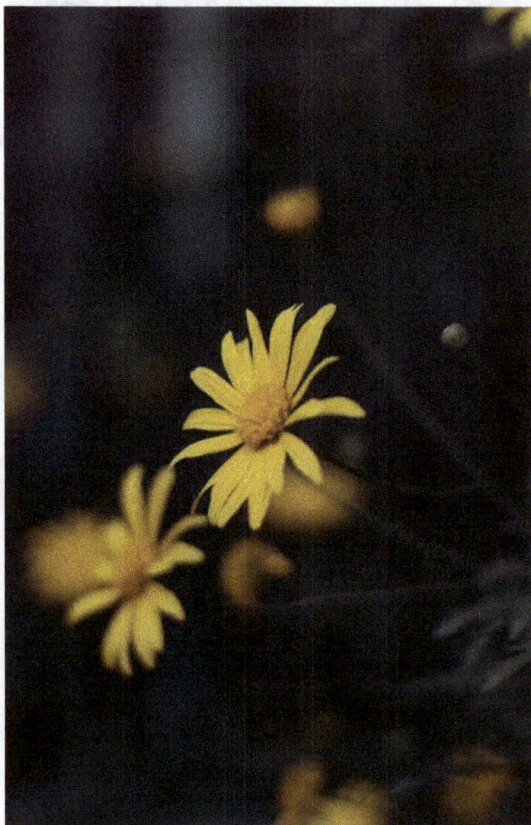

Arnica.[80]

- **Description:** Arnica is a yellow wildflower that grows low to the ground in the mountains and meadows. It has big, bright blooms that look like daisies on top of fuzzy green stems and leaves. The whole plant has an unforgettable, peppery smell when you squeeze the leaves or flowers. Arnica doesn't grow really tall, maybe reaching up to a foot high at most, but it spreads out and carpets the ground.

- **Therapeutic Properties:** Arnica made this list thanks to its active compounds, such as sesquiterpene lactones, which give it anti-inflammatory and pain-relieving effects.

- **Traditional Uses:** Arnica is used for muscle aches, joint pain, bruises, and other types of minor injuries and inflammation. It reduces swelling, and its astringent properties help treat skin irritations.

Sage

Sage.[81]

- **Description:** Sage is a minty herb that grows in tiny, shrubby bushes. It has soft, silvery-green leaves and small, purplish-blue flower spikes that bloom in the summer.

- **Therapeutic Properties:** Sage contains compounds like thujone, camphor, and rosmarinic acid, all of which have antimicrobial, anti-inflammatory, and antioxidant abilities.

- **Traditional Uses:** Sage is already recognized as a sacred plant because it is believed to purify the body, spirit, and spaces, but it also treats respiratory problems, digestive issues, memory problems, and skin conditions.

Valerian

Valerian.[82]

- **Description:** Valerian is a perennial plant with a long history as a natural remedy. It is a tall, flowering herb with large green leaves and pink/white summer flowers.

- **Therapeutic Properties:** The active compounds in valerian root, like valerenic acid, interact with the brain's GABA receptors, similar to how some prescription sleep medications work.

- **Traditional Uses:** Native American tribes relied on valerian to treat headaches, muscle cramps, and menstrual cramps. European herbalists also prescribed valerian for nervous disorders, heart palpitations, and other conditions linked to stress and anxiety.

Echinacea

Echinacea.[88]

- **Description:** Echinacea plants are another group of perennial herbs that grow one to three feet tall with sturdy, hairy stems and large daisy flower heads. The flowers generally have purple, pink, or white petals surrounding a spiky, copper-colored center cone. The types you'd see used for medicinal purposes are purple coneflower (Echinacea purpurea), narrow-leaf coneflower (Echinacea angustifolia), and pale purple coneflower (Echinacea pallida).

- **Therapeutic Properties:** The active compounds in echinacea – alkylamides and polysaccharides – seem to stimulate the production and activity of white blood cells. This strengthens the body's natural defenses against viruses, bacteria, and other pathogens. Echinacea also has some anti-inflammatory and antimicrobial properties. Some research suggests it may even help speed up the healing process for minor wounds and skin infections.

- **Traditional Uses:** Today, many people turn to echinacea at the first signs of a cold or flu to reduce the duration and severity of their symptoms. The roots and leaves were once used to treat snake bites, toothaches, sore throats, and skin infections.

Chamomile

Chamomile.[84]

- **Description:** Chamomile is an annual plant that grows close to the ground and only reaches about one foot in height. It has feathery, green-gray leaves and small flower heads made of white petals around a hollow, yellow center.

- **Therapeutic Properties:** Chamomile flowers contain compounds like apigenin that bind to certain receptors in the brain to produce a sedative and muscle-relaxing response.

- **Traditional Uses:** Chamomile is popular for stress relief, good sleep, and calming digestive issues like gas, bloating, and stomach cramps. It is also used on irritated skin to speed wound healing and to fight bacterial or fungal infections.

Oregon Grape

Oregon grape.[85]

- **Description:** The Oregon grape is an evergreen shrub standing two to six feet tall with leathery, spiny leaves that resemble holly. The leaves take on a beautiful reddish-purple tinge in the fall and bright yellow flowers in the summer. It also produces berries that start off green and mature to an inky blue-black color.

- **Therapeutic Properties:** The berberine in Oregon grape acts as a natural antibiotic to fight bacterial, viral, and fungal infections.

- **Traditional Uses:** Oregon grape supports the body's defenses against colds, flu, and other respiratory issues. It cleanses, detoxifies, and stimulates the production of bile for digestion and metabolism. The plant's anti-inflammatory mechanisms also make it great for skin conditions like eczema, psoriasis, and acne.

Peppermint

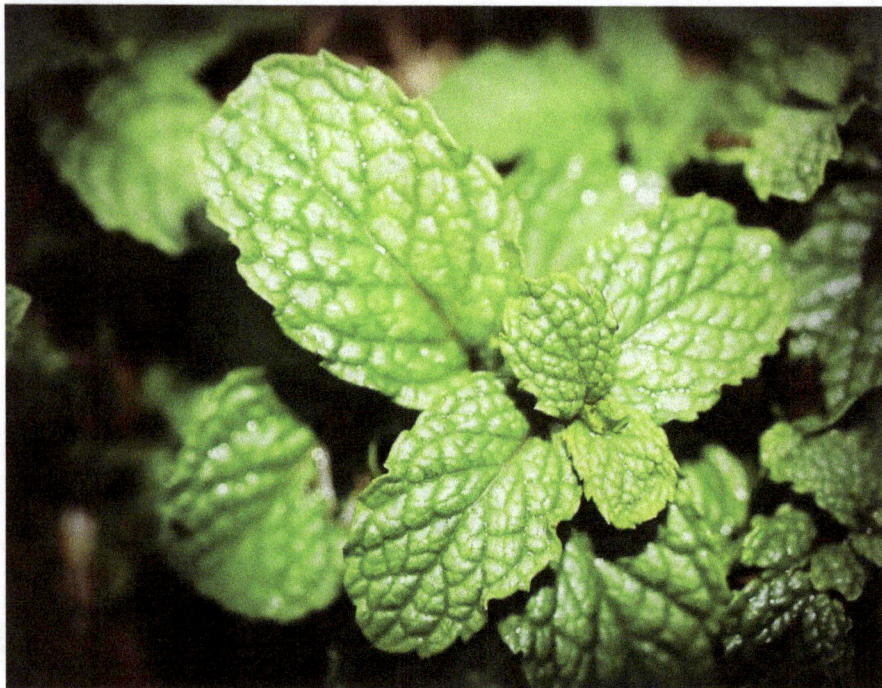

Peppermint.[86]

- **Description:** Peppermint is a natural hybrid of watermint and spearmint. Its stems are square and reddish-purple, with bright green, lance-shaped leaves that are rather crinkled. The plant grows one to two feet tall and produces small, pink, or lavender flowers in terminal spikes.

- **Therapeutic Properties:** Peppermint contains menthol, menthone, limonene, rosmarinic acid, carvone, and pulegone, among other plant compounds. The synergistic interactions between these plant compounds make peppermint so versatile and therapeutically potent.

- **Traditional Uses:** Drinking peppermint tea or taking peppermint supplements helps settle an upset stomach, reduces gas and bloating, and generally improves digestion. The menthol in peppermint is a natural antispasmodic, relaxing the gastrointestinal tract and letting food move through more easily.

Horsetail

Horsetail.[87]

- **Description:** Horsetail is a primitive plant that has existed for millions of years, predating even the dinosaurs. It is not a true flowering plant but rather a member of the Equisetaceae family – an ancient family of ferns.

- **Therapeutic Properties:** One standout feature of the horsetail plant is its high concentration of silica. Silica contributes to the formation and maintenance of strong, healthy connective tissues like bones, cartilage, tendons, and even nails. Horsetail also contains flavonoids and saponins, which are anti-inflammatory and antibacterial agents.

- **Traditional Uses:** Horsetail is a well-known diuretic. The plant's high silica content is believed to have a gentle yet potent effect on the urinary system, flushing out toxins and excess fluids. The plant's astringent properties contract blood vessels and slow the flow of blood. Some cultures would even apply the ground stems directly to the wound as a natural styptic.

Guidance and Tips

- **Proper Identification Is Important:** Before you go out foraging, you need to know that you can unquestionably identify the plants you're looking for. Many wild plants have lookalikes, some of which are toxic or dangerous. Do your research ahead of time, use field guides and trustworthy websites, and consult with experienced foragers or herbalists. If you have even the slightest doubt, leave that plant alone.

- **Sustainable Harvesting Practices:** Sustainable foraging applies to medicinal plants as well. Always be conscious of how much you're taking. Don't overharvest from a single area because that will damage or even kill the plant population. Instead, spread out your collection and only take what you need. Leave plenty behind for the plant to regenerate, and try not to damage the roots.

- **Ethical Considerations:** Foraging on public or private land requires respectful and responsible stewardship of the land. Get the necessary permission, follow all applicable laws and regulations, and leave no trace. Be considerate of sensitive ecosystems and endangered species and avoid them if possible. Also, understand that some plants may be culturally or spiritually significant to Indigenous communities, so research the local context before collecting anything.

Preparation Methods for Medicinal Plants

Drying

- **Air-drying:** Hanging or spreading the plant parts in a properly ventilated area with shade. This preserves the natural enzymatic activity.

- **Sun-drying:** Exposing the plants to direct sunlight, which is faster but may degrade some heat-sensitive compounds

- **Oven-drying:** Using a controlled-temperature oven, which allows for faster, more consistent drying

- **Freeze-drying:** Freezing the plants and then removing the water content through a process called lyophilization. This is best for volatile compounds.

Powdering

- **Grinding:** Reducing the dried plant material to a fine powder using mechanical grinders, mills, mortars, and pestles
- **Sieving:** Passing the ground powder through mesh sieves to get a uniform particle size

Extraction

- **Infusions:** Steeping the plant in hot water to extract water-soluble compounds, like in teas
- **Decoctions:** Boiling the plant in water to extract both water-soluble and some insoluble compounds
- **Tinctures:** Soaking the plant material in alcohol (or a water-alcohol mixture) to extract even more compounds
- **Essential oil distillation:** Using steam or hydro-distillation to vaporize and collect the volatile essential oils

Concentration

- **Evaporation:** Removing water from extracts through controlled heating or vacuum evaporation to increase the concentration of active compounds
- **Freeze-concentration:** Freezing the extract and then removing the ice crystals, leaving behind a more concentrated solution

Administration Methods for Medicinal Plants

Oral

- **Teas:** Infusions or decoctions of dried herbs, often taken hot
- **Tinctures:** Alcoholic extracts, typically taken by the dropperful
- **Capsules or tablets:** Dried, powdered herbs encapsulated or compressed into solid dosage tabs
- **Syrups:** Extracts or infusions mixed with a sweetener, like honey or glycerin

Topical

- **Ointments:** Plant extracts or essential oils mixed into a fatty base, like beeswax or petroleum jelly
- **Creams:** Water-in-oil or oil-in-water emulsions containing herbal extracts.

- **Salves:** Similar to ointments but with a softer, more spreadable consistency

- **Poultices:** Moist fresh or dried herbs wrapped in a cloth and applied directly to the affected skin

Inhalation

- **Steam inhalation:** Adding herbs to hot water and inhaling the steam

- **Smudging:** Burning dried herbs and inhaling the smoke

Safety Considerations and Potential Risks

- **Allergic Reactions:** Just like some people are allergic to peanuts or bee stings, certain herbs or plant compounds could trigger unwanted reactions in some people. These could range from mild skin irritation to asphyxiation. It's always smart to do a test run first, start with tiny amounts, and watch out for any strange symptoms.

- **Interactions with Medications:** Herbs are powerful, natural medicines, but they don't always play nicely with synthetic drugs. They can either amp up or cancel out the effects of prescription medications in unpredictable ways. If you're already taking something, always check with your doctor before adding any herbal remedies to your medication.

- **Dosage Guidelines:** When using herbs medicinally, more is not always better. The right herb will work wonders, but go overboard, and you could end up doing more harm than good. Factors like your size, age, and health status affect the ideal dose, so follow the instructions carefully, especially for children, the elderly, and expectant mothers.

- **Route of Administration:** The way you take an herb – whether you drink it, rub it on your skin, or breathe it in – all factors into how safe and effective it is. Some methods carry higher risks, like potentially damaging your liver if you swallow too much of certain herbs.

- **Cumulative Effects:** Taking herbal medicines long-term could cause certain compounds to build up in your body over time, potentially cascading problems down the line, so giving your system a break from them every so often is a good idea.

- **Interactions between Herbs:** Just like medications, different herbs react with each other in unexpected ways when you take them together. You have to be careful about mixing and matching because the combined effects might be more than you bargained for.

Herbalism is far from static. There's always something new to uncover about the complexity and versatility of plant-based medicines. Just when you think you know all there is to know about a plant, a new study comes along with never-before-seen properties or unexpected uses. That constant expansion of understanding is what makes herbalism one of the most fascinating and ever-evolving disciplines in existence. Each herb has so many facets – there's its chemical makeup, its complicated interactions, and its highly personalized effects. Truly grasping the full potential of a single plant could take years of dedicated study and hands-on experimentation. Add to that the thousands of species with documented medicinal uses, and the scope for investigation will blow your mind.

Don't see herbalism as a stagnant body of knowledge to memorize. Be curious and open to new information. Depending on how far you would like to go, you could take courses, attend workshops, or join online communities. It is possible to stay up-to-date with the latest research while also honoring the wisdom of Indigenous tribes. Herbalism is a living, breathing tradition, not just a set of remedies.

Chapter 8: Living a Foraging Lifestyle

Throughout the previous chapters, you've covered the fundamentals of foraging: identifying edible and medicinal plants, understanding seasonal availability, responsible foraging practices, etc, but this has been about so much more than just the technical skills. Foraging is a guiding principle for living. It's a primal relationship with the natural world and a lifestyle that teaches self-reliance, mindfulness, and appreciation for the abundance all around you.

You are in synchronicity with the rhythms of nature, a part of the holistic matrix of existence that sustains you.[88]

When you live as a forager, the filter that guides your understanding transforms along with you. You learn to slow down, attune your senses, read the nuanced signs of the seasons, and move through the earth with a hunter-gatherer's grace. You're not just collecting food anymore; you are in synchronicity with the rhythms of nature, a part of the holistic matrix of existence that sustains you.

In the spring, there's nothing quite like that first surge of fresh, green life after the long, slumbering winter, those first batches of greens - wild lettuces, nettles, and dandelion leaves. Foraging them is almost meditative as you slowly scan the ground, your eyes trained to spot the subtle differences that separate the edible from the poisonous. Then summer comes with wild strawberries, blackberries, and raspberries practically falling off the bushes, begging to be eaten. Going into the forests during the fall, the relationships between all the plants, animals, and fungi are clearer than they've ever been. That fallen log isn't just dead wood; it's an entire community, a mini-ecosystem unto itself - a home to countless insects, fungi, and decomposers all working together to return the wood to the soil.

Then comes the quieter, inward-turning season of winter. To a non-initiate, the landscape may appear dormant on the surface, but beneath the snow and bare branches, life is still moving and changing. The trees are resting, conserving their energy for the next season of growth. Small animals burrow into the earth or hunker down in their dens, their metabolisms slowing to a crawl as they wait out the cold. It's a time of stillness and introspection, a time to reflect on the cycle of the seasons and your place within them. The patterns of nature have become your own, and you wouldn't have it any other way.

The Implications of a Foraging Lifestyle

With your newfound commitment to foraging, you might be surprised by just how much it can change your life for the better. Ditching the processed junk and reconnecting with the natural foods in your own backyard puts you on a path toward a healthier way of living. One of the first things you'll probably notice is how much better you feel on the inside. The more you fill your plate with wild-foraged plants, berries, and mushrooms, the more you give your body all it's been missing - vitamins, minerals, antioxidants, etc. You won't be worried about bloating and energy crashes from ultra-processed foods, not when you're feeling light, energized, and maybe even a little superhuman. Your skin will look brighter and clearer, your hair will become shinier, and you might even lose a few pounds without even trying.

Foraging is also a way to give back to the planet. The industrial food system is a mess. Massive monoculture farms, toxic pesticides, and resource-guzzling factory farms are devastating natural landscapes, but as a forager, you've opted out of that destructive system altogether. You're not clearing away entire ecosystems to grow a single crop; you're carefully and sustainably gathering only the wild plants, berries, and mushrooms that you need, *the way humans have done for thousands of years.* This gentleness and thoughtfulness keep these natural spaces alive to still provide food and shelter for all the plants and animals that live there. You're not just taking; you're also giving back.

Gathering around the table and sharing a meal made with ingredients you all picked with your own two hands is such a bonding experience.[89]

With foraging, you're part of the solution, not the problem.

Foraging could also connect you with your local community. When you're out there in the woods or fields, you're bound to run into other people doing the same thing, and once you get to know a few of those fellow foragers, the possibilities really start to open up. Before you know it, you're hosting a big community potluck, where everyone brings the edibles they've gathered. Just imagine the spread: fresh berries, herbs, greens, maybe even some sautéed mushrooms or elderberry jam. Gathering around the table and sharing a meal made with ingredients you all picked with your own two hands is such a bonding experience. Something about it feels more intimate and meaningful than a standard dinner party. Besides, you get to learn from each other. Maybe someone knows a secret recipe for preparing stinging nettles, or someone else found the best spot for boletes.

If you somehow never run into other foragers while you're out, why not see if there's a foraging group or club in your neighborhood? You could learn from experienced foragers, swap tips, and make some nature-loving friends in the process. Besides, going on group outings is always more fun (and safer) than striking out alone. If you're more of the independent type, taking a hands-on foraging workshop could be more your thing. You'll get to do some guided learning and fieldwork with an expert guide, which will be immensely helpful for sharpening your identification skills. Of course, nothing beats simply spending more time in nature on your own. The more you get out there and give your foraging skills a go, the better you'll get at developing that forager's eye.

Tips for Integrating Foraged Foods into Everyday Life

- Use wild greens like dandelion, chickweed, or lambsquarters in your salads, stir-fries, or as a quick sauté. They have way more nutrients than your typical greens.

- Use the petals of nasturtiums, calendulas, or wild roses to make floral syrups or infused oils.

- Forage for wild onions, chives, or wild garlic, and use them just like you would the cultivated versions.

- Dry out your wild greens, herbs, and flowers so you can use them in teas or as seasonings.

- Make syrups, shrubs, or fermented drinks from wild berries, flowers, or fruits so you can have the flavors more often than they are in season.

- Pickle or ferment any extra wild mushrooms or greens to preserve them for later.

- Substitute new wild ingredients into your go-to recipes.

- Use wild rose hips to make a tangy vitamin C jelly that pairs amazingly with cheese and crackers.

- Dehydrate wild mushrooms and grind them into a seasoning powder.

- Make a wild green soup using nettles, lambsquarters, and wild mustard greens as the base.

- Make a wild berry vinaigrette using serviceberries, currants, or gooseberries for a salad dressing.

- Dry and grind sumac berries into a lemony spice for rubs, dressings, or seasonings.

The Importance of Sharing Your Knowledge and Experience

There's a saying that goes, "Knowledge is power," but an even more important truth is that knowledge is meant to be shared. How many times have you learned something new - it doesn't have to be related to foraging; it could just be a fascinating bit of trivia - and you couldn't wait to tell your friends or family about it? That impulse to share what you know is natural because, at the end of the day, keeping information to yourself doesn't do much good.

Have you gone foraging at all before? Maybe a friend took you, or you went with your mom. Wasn't it amazing to learn which plants were safe to eat and which ones to avoid? It must've felt like a light bulb moment. In times like these, it doesn't feel right to just hoard that knowledge; you'll want to pass it on so others can experience that same wonder and self-sufficiency.

Forget practical skills; even your personal experiences and perspectives are gifts to share with people. How many times have you gone through something, only to realize later on that your story could really help someone else going through a similar thing? Or perhaps you picked up a new hobby that you just can't stop talking about because you're so excited about it. Sharing what you know and what you've been through is a gift. It connects you to others, you teach, and you learn, and you inspire and are inspired. It doesn't have to be anything big or grandiose - even the tiniest bits of information could be everything to someone else. People who are humble enough to admit what they don't know but generous enough to share what they do know are the ones who make the best communities.

Foraging connects you to people and nature.[90]

Community or not, at the end of the day, foraging is more than free food. Your connection to the land is fundamental to who you are as a human being. The land is not just a backdrop or resource but the very foundation upon which life, culture, and societies are built. It's where your roots are literally and figuratively grounded. In a time of increasing disconnection and environmental upheaval, the future of the planet depends on people like you who are willing to tread lightly, live purposefully, and leave each place you visit in better condition than you found it. This is the promise and the sacred duty of the foraging life.

Bonus: Mountain West Foraging Calendar

Mountain West Foraging Calendar

❄ Winter / 🌱 Spring / ☀ Summer / 🍀 Fall	Jan	Feb	Mar	Apr	May	Jun	Jul	Aug	Sep	Oct	Nov	Dec
🌱 SPRING												
Wild onions			●	●	●	●						
Dandelion roots			●	●	●	●			●	●		
Horsetail			●	●	●	●						
Morel mushroom			●	●	●	●						
Dandelion				●	●					●		
Stinging nettles				●	●	●						
Watercress				●	●							
Chives			●	●	●	●						
Chickweed					●	●				●	●	
Lambsquaters					●	●			●			
Miners lettuce					●					●	●	
Wild mustard greens					●							
Violets					●	●						
Pansies					●	●						
Wild roses					●	●	●					
Elderflower					●	●						
Serviceberries					●	●						
Currants					●	●		●				
Camas lily					●	●	●					

	Winter	Spring	Summer	Fall	Jan	Feb	Mar	Apr	May	Jun	Jul	Aug	Sep	Oct	Nov	Dec
Nasturtiums			☀							☀						
Fireweed										■	■	■	☀			
Strawberry									■	■	☀					
Chia seeds										■	■	☀				
Yarrow										■	■	☀				
Arnica										■	■	☀				
Sage										■	■	☀				
Chamomile										■	■	☀				
Coral mushrooms										☀		■	☀			
Shaggymane mushrooms										☀			■	☀		
Purslane											■	☀				
Sunflower											■	■	☀			
Huckleberries											■	☀				
Raspberries											■	■	☀			
Valerian											■	☀				
Peppermint											■	☀				
Boletes											■	■	☀			
Lobster mushrooms											■	■	☀			
Chokecherries												■	☀			
Acorns												■	■	■	■	☀

	Jan	Feb	Mar	Apr	May	Jun	Jul	Aug	Sep	Oct	Nov	Dec
❄ Winter ☘ Spring ☀ Summer 🍂 Fall												
Pecan								☀	☀			
Evening primrose								☀	☀	☀		
Wild carrot roots								☀	☀	☀		
Echinacea							☀	☀				
Oyster mushrooms								☀	☀	☀		
Porcini								☀	☀			
Matsutake								☀	☀	☀		
Cauliflower mushrooms								☀				
Chicken-of-the-woods								☀	☀	☀		

🍂 FALL

	Jan	Feb	Mar	Apr	May	Jun	Jul	Aug	Sep	Oct	Nov	Dec
Pine nuts									🍂	🍂		
Hazelnut									🍂			
Juniperberry									🍂	🍂		
Black walnuts									🍂			
Burdock								🍂	🍂			
Sunchokes									🍂	🍂		
Oregon grape									🍂			
Hazelnut										🍂		

Index: A-Z of Wild Edibles, Mushrooms, and Medicinal Plants

Conclusion

If you've made it this far, you're well on your way to becoming an accomplished forager. The knowledge and skills you've gained from this book are only just the beginning. As you get out there and put them into practice, you'll find that foraging is a constantly evolving pursuit - there's always more to learn, more to discover.

One of the best parts of foraging is how it connects you to the cultural roots of the Indigenous peoples who have lived in this region for what seems like forever. Many of the plants you learned about have been essential foods and medicines for the Native American tribes of this region for generation after generation. It's humbling to realize that the same plants you put in your basket have fed and healed the first peoples of this land for thousands of years.

Even if you don't have a personal or family history tied to the Mountain West, foraging can still tap into that ancient instinct inside of you. There's just something about picking wild foods and medicines that make you feel reconnected to the natural world in a deep, somewhat ancestral way. It's like your body and mind are remembering a relationship with the land that has been buried under all the noise and busyness of modern urban life. Foraging and harnessing wild resources was once the way of life, and even though most people don't need to do that to stay alive today, there's still a part of you that yearns for that direct, primitive connection.

As you continue foraging, get a journal or notebook and use it to meticulously document the plants you find. Draw pictures of them, and write down exactly where you found them and any information you learn about their edible or medicinal uses. It might feel like homework, but this is how you'll really cement that plant knowledge in your brain. This journal is going to become an invaluable personal reference that you can keep coming back to. You'll be able to flip through and quickly refresh your memory on that weird-looking green thing you found last spring or remember the place where you found all those shaggy manes. All that information in one place will save you so much time and frustration.

The joy of foraging isn't just in the end result; it's in the entire process, from the quiet observation to the patient identification to the hands-on harvesting. Try not to rush through it! Slow down, pay attention, and let yourself get lost in the magic of it all. It's in those moments of intimate engagement that foraging becomes more than just a means to an end.

The joy is in *everything else.*

Here's another book by Dion Rosser
that you might like

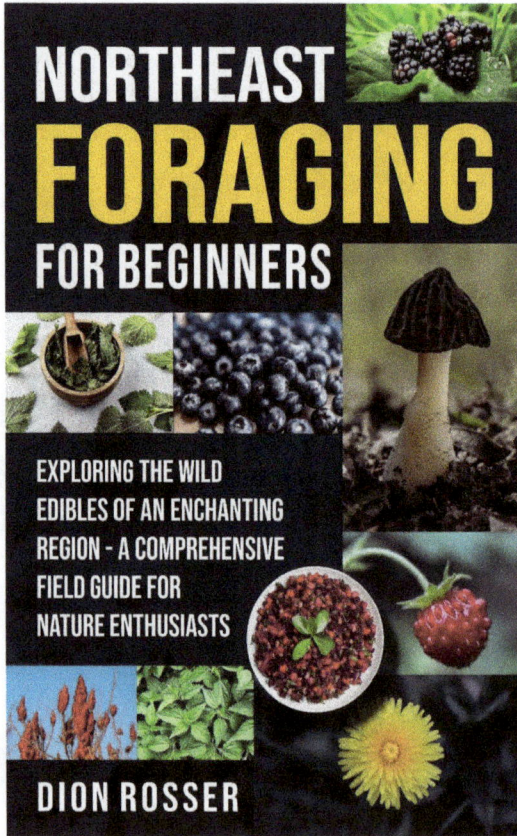

NORTHEAST FORAGING FOR BEGINNERS

EXPLORING THE WILD EDIBLES OF AN ENCHANTING REGION - A COMPREHENSIVE FIELD GUIDE FOR NATURE ENTHUSIASTS

DION ROSSER

References

Alan. (n.d.). Types of Edible Wild Mushrooms Archives. FORAGER | CHEF. https://foragerchef.com/category/wild-mushroom-species/

An, M. (2023, August 23). Foraging for Edible Coral Mushrooms. Project Upland. https://projectupland.com/foraging/picking-coral-mushrooms/

Aon, O. (2020, April 23). Oyster Mushrooms, Pleurotus Species. Forage Colorado. https://www.foragecolorado.com/post/oyster-mushrooms-pleurotus-species

Bailey, L. (2003, April 1). Echinacea: What Should I Know About It? Familydoctor.org. https://familydoctor.org/echinacea-what-should-i-know-about-it/

Codekas, C. (2021, February 26). Foraging for Wild Violets: an Edible Early Spring Flower. Grow Forage Cook Ferment. https://www.growforagecookferment.com/foraging-for-wild-violets/

Derr, A. (2023, April 2). 27 Amazing Animals in Rocky Mountain National Park | The Next Summit: a Mountain Blog. Www.thenextsummit.org. https://thenextsummit.org/animals-in-rocky-mountain-national-park/#google_vignette

Keough, B. (2020, July 13). Here's What You'll Need to Start Foraging Mushrooms. Wirecutter: Reviews for the Real World. https://www.nytimes.com/wirecutter/blog/how-to-hunt-mushrooms/

Lambert, R. (2018, December 20). Foraging as a Way to Feel Connected. Wild Walks Southwest. https://www.wildwalks-southwest.co.uk/foraging-as-a-way-to-feel-connected/

Oder, T. (2022, September 1). Identifying Wild Mushrooms: a Guide to Edible and Poisonous Mushrooms. Treehugger. https://www.treehugger.com/wild-mushrooms-what-to-eat-what-to-avoid-4864324

Pickled Wild Onions. (2013, June 21). The Cookery Maven. https://www.thecookerymaven.com/cookery-maven-blog/2013/06/pickled-wild-onions

Sayner, A. (2019, May 13). A Complete Guide to Oyster Mushrooms - GroCycle. GroCycle. https://grocycle.com/oyster-mushrooms-guide/

Image Sources

[1] *designed by Freepik. https://www.freepik.com/free-photo/gardener_3572143.htm*

[2] *Chrysaora on Flickr, CC BY 2.0 <https://creativecommons.org/licenses/by/2.0>, via Wikimedia Commons. https://commons.wikimedia.org/wiki/File:Picea_engelmannii_foliage_cones2.jpg*

[3] *designed by Freepik. https://www.freepik.com/free-photo/young-farmer-holding-basket-with-vegetables-from-his-farm_21076582.htm*

[4] *designed by Freepik. https://www.freepik.com/free-photo/reforestation-done-by-voluntary-group_29015531.htm*

[5] *Pittigrilli, CC BY 4.0 <https://creativecommons.org/licenses/by/4.0>, via Wikimedia Commons. https://commons.wikimedia.org/wiki/File:Pocket_knive_(penknife)_from_German_bicycle_retailer_Polo.jpg*

[6] *W.carter, CC BY-SA 4.0 <https://creativecommons.org/licenses/by-sa/4.0>, via Wikimedia Commons. https://commons.wikimedia.org/wiki/File:Beetroots_in_a_basket.jpg*

[7] *Wodgester, CC BY-SA 4.0 <https://creativecommons.org/licenses/by-sa/4.0>, via Wikimedia Commons. https://commons.wikimedia.org/wiki/File:Compass_on_map.jpg*

[8] *barockschloss from Zeilitzheim, Germany, CC BY 2.0 <https://creativecommons.org/licenses/by/2.0>, via Wikimedia Commons. https://commons.wikimedia.org/wiki/File:Pruning_shears.jpg*

[9] *PumpkinSky, CC BY-SA 4.0 <https://creativecommons.org/licenses/by-sa/4.0>, via Wikimedia Commons. https://commons.wikimedia.org/wiki/File:Work_glove_for_right_hand_LR.jpg*

[10] *Mersaleashwaran, CC BY-SA 4.0 <https://creativecommons.org/licenses/by-sa/4.0>, via Wikimedia Commons. https://commons.wikimedia.org/wiki/File:Zooming_a_plant_with_magnifying_glass.jpg*

[26] George F Mayfield, CC BY-SA 2.0 <https://creativecommons.org/licenses/by-sa/2.0>, via Wikimedia Commons https://commons.wikimedia.org/wiki/File:Allium_canadense_WILD_ONION.jpg

[27] Tubifex, CC BY-SA 3.0 <https://creativecommons.org/licenses/by-sa/3.0>, via Wikimedia Commons https://upload.wikimedia.org/wikipedia/commons/c/c8/3853_-_Tropaeolum_majus_%28Gro%C3%9Fe_Kapuzinerkresse%29.JPG

[28] H. Zell, CC BY-SA 3.0 <https://creativecommons.org/licenses/by-sa/3.0>, via Wikimedia Commons. https://commons.wikimedia.org/wiki/File:Viola_reichenbachiana_001.jpg

[29] Mountain pansy (Viola lutea) above Swindale Wood by Andrew Curtis, CC BY-SA 2.0 <https://creativecommons.org/licenses/by-sa/2.0>, via Wikimedia Commons. https://commons.wikimedia.org/wiki/File:Mountain_pansy_(Viola_lutea)_above_Swindale_Wood_-_geograph.org.uk_-_2425313.jpg

[30] Sanjay Acharya, CC BY-SA 4.0 <https://creativecommons.org/licenses/by-sa/4.0>, via Wikimedia Commons. https://commons.wikimedia.org/wiki/File:Dandelion_Flower_close_up.jpg

[31] https://commons.wikimedia.org/wiki/File:Sunflowers_helianthus_annuus.jpg

[32] James St. John, CC BY 2.0 <https://creativecommons.org/licenses/by/2.0>, via Wikimedia Commons https://upload.wikimedia.org/wikipedia/commons/2/29/Rosa_woodsii_%28Wood%27s_rose%29_%28Gibbon_Falls_overlook%2C_Yellowstone%2C_Wyoming%2C_USA%29_1_%2820799206725%29.jpg

[33] J Brew, CC BY-SA 2.0 <https://creativecommons.org/licenses/by-sa/2.0>, via Wikimedia Commons https://upload.wikimedia.org/wikipedia/commons/5/57/Sambucus_cerulea_Brewton_Road.jpg

[34] https://upload.wikimedia.org/wikipedia/commons/d/df/Cicuta_maculata.jpg

[35] H. Zell, CC BY-SA 3.0 <https://creativecommons.org/licenses/by-sa/3.0>, via Wikimedia Commons. https://commons.wikimedia.org/wiki/File:Allium_schoenoprasum_001.JPG

[36] Agnieszka Kwiecień, Nova, CC BY-SA 4.0 <https://creativecommons.org/licenses/by-sa/4.0>, via Wikimedia Commons https://commons.wikimedia.org/wiki/File:Chamerion_angustifolium_Wierzb%C3%B3wka_kiprzyca_2023-08-22_Dolina_Ko%C5%9Bcieliska_07.jpg

[37] Jörg Hempel, CC BY-SA 3.0 DE <https://creativecommons.org/licenses/by-sa/3.0/de/deed.en>, via Wikimedia Commons https://upload.wikimedia.org/wikipedia/commons/6/64/Fragaria_vesca_LC0389.jpg

[38] Robert Flogaus-Faust, CC BY 4.0 <https://creativecommons.org/licenses/by/4.0>, via Wikimedia Commons https://upload.wikimedia.org/wikipedia/commons/1/10/Potentilla_indica_RF.jpg

[39] Krzysztof Ziarnek, Kenraiz, CC BY-SA 4.0 <https://creativecommons.org/licenses/by-sa/4.0>, via Wikimedia Commons. https://commons.wikimedia.org/wiki/File:Amelanchier_alnifolia_kz09.jpg

[40] waferboard, CC BY 2.0 <https://creativecommons.org/licenses/by/2.0>, via Wikimedia Commons. https://commons.wikimedia.org/wiki/File:Green_Timbers_tart_huckleberries_(6008182409).jpg

[41] Robert Flogaus-Faust, CC BY 4.0 <https://creativecommons.org/licenses/by/4.0>, via Wikimedia Commons https://upload.wikimedia.org/wikipedia/commons/e/e2/Rubus_idaeus_3_RF.jpg

⁴² *Frank Vincentz, CC BY-SA 3.0 <http://creativecommons.org/licenses/by-sa/3.0/>, via Wikimedia Commons https://upload.wikimedia.org/wikipedia/commons/2/24/Rubus_fruticosus_14_ies.jpg*

⁴³ *https://upload.wikimedia.org/wikipedia/commons/2/2e/File-Ribes_aureum_-_native%3B-Alternate_names-_Buffalo_currant%2C_clove_currant%2C_Missouri_currant%3B-Blooms_April_-_May%3B-This_plant_is_%280be4cf15-41ad-494f-9b6a-21c63c2754ae%29.JPG*

⁴⁴ *Maxime Laterreur, CC BY-SA 4.0 <https://creativecommons.org/licenses/by-sa/4.0>, via Wikimedia Commons. https://commons.wikimedia.org/wiki/File:Cerisier_de_Virginie_(Prunus_virginiana).jpg*

⁴⁵ *Famartin, CC BY-SA 4.0 <https://creativecommons.org/licenses/by-sa/4.0>, via Wikimedia Commons https://commons.wikimedia.org/wiki/File:2015-09-27_11_37_07_Colorado_pinyon_pine_cones_with_ripe_pine_nuts_at_the_Devil%27s_Canyon_Overlook_along_Interstate_70_in_Emery_County,_Utah.jpg*

⁴⁶ *Superior National Forest, CC BY 2.0 <https://creativecommons.org/licenses/by/2.0>, via Wikimedia Commons https://upload.wikimedia.org/wikipedia/commons/4/47/Corylus_americana_3-eheep_%285097498779%29.jpg*

⁴⁷ *Brad Haire, University of Georgia, USA, CC BY 3.0 US <https://creativecommons.org/licenses/by/3.0/us/deed.en>, via Wikimedia Commons. https://commons.wikimedia.org/wiki/File:Carya_illinoinensis_foliagenuts.jpg*

⁴⁸ *Jarek Tuszyński / CC-BY-SA-3.0, CC BY-SA 3.0 <https://creativecommons.org/licenses/by-sa/3.0>, via Wikimedia Commons https://upload.wikimedia.org/wikipedia/commons/d/d4/Joshua_Tree_National_Park_flowers_-_Salvia_columbariae_-_8.JPG*

⁴⁹ *Chris Light, CC BY-SA 4.0 <https://creativecommons.org/licenses/by-sa/4.0>, via Wikimedia Commons. https://commons.wikimedia.org/wiki/File:Juniper_berries_1776.jpg*

⁵⁰ *Chris Light, CC BY-SA 4.0 <https://creativecommons.org/licenses/by-sa/4.0>, via Wikimedia Commons. https://commons.wikimedia.org/wiki/File:Black_walnut_(Juglans_nigra)9817.jpg*

⁵¹ *Laval University, CC BY-SA 4.0 <https://creativecommons.org/licenses/by-sa/4.0>, via Wikimedia Commons https://upload.wikimedia.org/wikipedia/commons/3/35/Arctium_lappa_15-p.bot-arcti.lappa-20.jpg*

⁵² *https://upload.wikimedia.org/wikipedia/commons/6/69/Camassia_quamash_%28Pursh%29_Greene.jpg*

⁵³ *https://commons.wikimedia.org/wiki/File:Death_camas_Zygadenus_venenosus_3_(18466934961).jpg*

⁵⁴ *Charles de Mille-Isles from Mille-Isles, Canada, CC BY 2.0 <https://creativecommons.org/licenses/by/2.0>, via Wikimedia Commons. https://commons.wikimedia.org/wiki/File:Evening_primrose_-_Oenothera_biennis_(5991581156).jpg*

⁵⁵ *Leonora (Ellie) Enking from East Preston, United Kingdom, CC BY-SA 2.0 <https://creativecommons.org/licenses/by-sa/2.0>, via Wikimedia Commons https://commons.wikimedia.org/wiki/File:Daucus_carota_(28698897272).jpg*

⁵⁶ *https://commons.wikimedia.org/wiki/File:Dandelion_root.jpg*

[57] https://www.pexels.com/photo/shallow-focus-photography-of-mushrooms-1643422/

[58] Koshur, CC BY-SA 4.0 <https://creativecommons.org/licenses/by-sa/4.0>, via Wikimedia Commons. https://commons.wikimedia.org/wiki/File:Morel_mushrooms.jpg

[59] https://commons.wikimedia.org/wiki/File:Gyromitra_tasmanica_False_morel._(26258556133).jpg

[60] Chiring Chandan, CC BY-SA 4.0 <https://creativecommons.org/licenses/by-sa/4.0>, via Wikimedia Commons. https://commons.wikimedia.org/wiki/File:Pleurotus_ostreatus_(Oyster_Mushroom)_1.jpg

[61] John.Chy, Copyrighted free use, via Wikimedia Commons https://upload.wikimedia.org/wikipedia/commons/2/28/Omphalotus_olearius_in_NE_IL.JPG

[62] Holger Krisp, CC BY 3.0 <https://creativecommons.org/licenses/by/3.0>, via Wikimedia Commons. https://commons.wikimedia.org/wiki/File:(Gemeine_Steinpilz)_Boletus_edulis.jpg

[63] This image was created by user Ron Pastorino (Ronpast) at Mushroom Observer, a source for mycological images.You can contact this user here.English | español | français | italiano | македонски | മലയാളം | português | +/−, CC BY-SA 3.0 <https://creativecommons.org/licenses/by-sa/3.0>, via Wikimedia Commons https://commons.wikimedia.org/wiki/File:2012-11-21_Boletus_eastwoodiae_(Murrill)_Sacc._%26_Trotter_285505.jpg

[64] Tomomarusan, CC BY-SA 3.0 <http://creativecommons.org/licenses/by-sa/3.0/>, via Wikimedia Commons. https://commons.wikimedia.org/wiki/File:Matsutake.jpg

[65] https://commons.wikimedia.org/wiki/File:Amanita_phalloides_2011_G2.jpg

[66] Jerzy Opioła, CC BY-SA 3.0 <https://creativecommons.org/licenses/by-sa/3.0>, via Wikimedia Commons https://upload.wikimedia.org/wikipedia/commons/2/2f/Artomyces_pyxidatus_G3.jpg

[67] This image was created by user Robert(the 3 foragers) (the 3foragers) at Mushroom Observer, a source for mycological images. You can contact this user here. English | español | français | italiano | македонски | മലയാളം | português | +/−, CC BY-SA 3.0 <https://creativecommons.org/licenses/by-sa/3.0>, via Wikimedia Commons. https://commons.wikimedia.org/wiki/File:Sebacina_schweinitzii_(Peck)_Oberw_906735.jpg

[68] Daderot, CC0, via Wikimedia Commons. https://commons.wikimedia.org/wiki/File:Lobster_mushrooms_-_San_Francisco,_CA.jpg

[69] Alexis, CC BY 4.0 <https://creativecommons.org/licenses/by/4.0>, via Wikimedia Commons https://upload.wikimedia.org/wikipedia/commons/7/7c/Sparassis_crispa_103223639.jpg

[70] David R.York, CC BY-SA 4.0 <https://creativecommons.org/licenses/by-sa/4.0>, via Wikimedia Commons. https://commons.wikimedia.org/wiki/File:Shaggy_Mane_mushrooms.jpg

[71] https://commons.wikimedia.org/wiki/File:Destroying_Angel_02.jpg

[72] Agnes Monkelbaan, CC BY-SA 4.0 <https://creativecommons.org/licenses/by-sa/4.0>, via Wikimedia Commons. https://commons.wikimedia.org/wiki/File:Locatie,_Hortus_(Haren,_Groningen)._Laetiporus_sulphureus.jpg

[73] Matej Frančeškin, CC BY 4.0 <https://creativecommons.org/licenses/by/4.0>, via Wikimedia Commons. https://commons.wikimedia.org/wiki/File:GalrinaMarginata.jpg

[74] https://www.pexels.com/photo/vegetable-salad-3026808/

[75] https://www.pexels.com/photo/pancakes-on-plate-17500013/

[76] https://www.pexels.com/photo/white-ceramic-bowl-with-mushroom-soup-4103375/

[77] https://www.pexels.com/photo/jar-of-chia-seed-pudding-with-almond-flakes-and-blueberries-4397288/

[78] https://www.pexels.com/photo/a-woman-holding-basket-full-of-lavender-flowers-5126994/

[79] https://www.pexels.com/photo/white-cluster-flowers-in-bloom-1408213/

[80] https://www.pexels.com/photo/yellow-arnica-flower-19116842/

[81] https://www.pexels.com/photo/close-up-photo-of-dried-sage-6103379/

[82] https://www.pexels.com/photo/close-up-photo-of-flowering-valerian-plants-17247500/

[83] https://www.pexels.com/photo/tender-echinacea-purpurea-with-white-petals-in-garden-5242298/

[84] https://www.pexels.com/photo/shallow-focus-photography-of-yellow-and-white-flowers-during-daytime-159110/

[85] https://www.pexels.com/photo/close-up-of-a-flowering-oregon-grape-16581419/

[86] https://www.pexels.com/photo/green-mint-photo-214165/

[87] MPF, CC BY-SA 3.0 <https://creativecommons.org/licenses/by-sa/3.0>, via Wikimedia Commons. https://commons.wikimedia.org/wiki/File:Equisetum_arvense_foliage.jpg

[88] https://www.pexels.com/photo/unrecognizable-farmer-harvesting-red-coffee-berries-in-forest-7125531/

[89] https://www.pexels.com/photo/diverse-female-gardeners-harvesting-fruits-in-garden-6231704/

[90] https://www.pexels.com/photo/gardener-harvesting-apples-with-daughter-in-garden-5528990/